My hope is that the reader will begin to practice and pray for total and complete deliverance from those strongholds that are keeping them from living their lives to the fullest through our Lord Jesus Christ.

—Sean F. Brennan
Station Manager, WNYB-TV
Orchard Park, New York

What Others Are Saying

It's time for the church to take a good hard look at demons and the deliverance ministry. Jesus ministered deliverance. He said His disciples would also. The world needs to experience deliverance. People want to be set free from their bondages and addictions. We can set them free in Jesus name, if we understand the principles of deliverance ministry. *Miraculously Set Free* will give you an excellent understanding of what deliverance is and how to cast demons out of a tormented individual. The church owes the world an encounter with God. Let's provide them that.

—Dr. Mark Virkler President,
Communion With God Ministries

Miraculously Set Free written by Pastor Mary Ellen Gordon is a book that should be read by all, who are struggling with life's problems without seeing the cause nor the answer. It is a way to realize that "Deliverance" is not a bad word, nor one to be feared. Pastor Gordon gives a simple, concise way of understanding how we got where we are and how to be free of our difficulties and problems, through the name of Jesus and the power that is in that name to free us from all bondage. Whether you are a mature Christian, or a Babe in Christ, it's a book you need to read. A truthful, easy, simple application through the Word of God, that will change your life.

—Pastor Don Schiemant
Director of the Healing Rooms of Buffalo Niagara
Buffalo, New York

Miraculously Set Free is an enlightening read of the promises of God based upon the premise of 'If the Son therefore shall make you free, ye shall be free indeed'. (John 8:36). Here the believer is called to walk in the gift of faith, understanding that as there is an abiding in the power of the word, therein lies your divine source of hope, strength and liberty in Christ Jesus.

—Pastor Simeon Strauser
Chairman, Full Gospel Assemblies
Parkesburg, Pennsylvania

Hope is a very powerful word to our human existence. We hope our family and friends are healthy and safe, we hope for our political future, we hope for our finances. But hope is even more powerful for Christians whose hope is in our Lord Jesus Christ to help cover every area of their lives.

Mary Ellen Gordon's *Miraculously Set Free* brings these hopes to be set free into a teaching format that gives the reader a road map from the foundation through Jesus to the practical application within our everyday lives. One or two of the prayers will be taped to my mirror as a touchstone and a daily reminder of whose I am, Jesus.

Miraculously Set Free

A Guide to Experiencing
Personal Deliverance

Mary Ellen Gordon

Gotham Books

30 N Gould St.
Ste. 20820, Sheridan, WY 82801
https://gothambooksinc.com/

Phone: 1 (307) 464-7800

© 2025 *Mary Ellen Gordon*. All rights reserved.

No part of this book may be reproduced, stored in a retrieval system, or transmitted by any means without the written permission of the author.

Published by Gotham Books (April 23, 2025)

ISBN: 979-8-3482-6923-4 (P)
ISBN: 979-8-3482-6924-1 (E)

Because of the dynamic nature of the Internet, any web addresses or links contained in this book may have changed since publication and may no longer be valid.

The views expressed in this work are solely those of the author and do not necessarily reflect the views of the publisher, and the publisher hereby disclaims any responsibility for them.

Dedication

To my heavenly Father, my Lord Jesus Christ and Holy Spirit who have imparted to me their passion and great compassion for all who are struggling with some form of bondage and are in need of deliverance.

To the church, the body of Christ, who is greatly in need of this revelation so that all of God's people will walk in their full inheritance in Christ—healing, divine health, freedom from all bondage, safety, provision, and protection, prosperity, and blessings in every area of their lives.

To all who suffer with sickness and disease, and every form of torment and oppression from the devil.

To every seeking soul who knows that "there's got to be more," and are willing to do whatever it takes to obtain the healing and deliverance they so desperately need.

To all who seek to know "the truth" concerning personal deliverance for themselves and others.

To all who desire to be equipped to go forward in fulfilling the "great commission" which God has given to every believer in Christ—to win the lost, heal the sick, and set every captive free.

To my board of trustees, ministry prayer partners, and all who have supported me in this project, and *Waves of Glory Miracle Ministries* since its inception.

Contents

Preface 1
Prologue 3
Introduction 9

Chapter 1 Jesus's Deliverance Ministry 13
Chapter 2 Do Demons Really Exist? 23
Chapter 3 What is Deliverance? 32
Chapter 4 Can a Christian Have a Demon? 38
Chapter 5 Can An Unsaved Person Be Delivered? 49
Chapter 6 Oppression or Possession? 55
Chapter 7 The Authority of Every Believer 63
Chapter 8 Dealing with Strongholds 76
Chapter 9 Generational Curses 83
Chapter 10 Deliverance from Ungodly Soul Ties 95
Chapter 11 Guidelines for Deliverance 100
Chapter 12 Expectations for Deliverance 112
Chapter 13 The Process of Self-Deliverance 124
Chapter 14 Maintaining Your Deliverance 146

Deliverance Prayers 165
Deliverance Questionnaire 172
Bibliography 177
About the Author 179

Preface

*And it is the Spirit that beareth witness,
because the Spirit is truth.*

1 John 5:6

There seems to be a growing *sense of urgency* and increased interest in deliverance ministry in recent years—not just in third world countries where it is more widely accepted, but even here in the West. It seems that some people groups that we may consider primitive—often have a greater awareness of the world of the supernatural than much of the "church" as we know it today. We're finding that desperate people are increasingly recognizing their need for deliverance from the power of evil spirits that have brought torment and oppression into their lives.

Many are beginning to take a second look at this much-needed ministry, which was known and practiced by the first century church. Confronting demons and casting them out was not uncommon among the people—resulting in many being set free from every form of bondage of the soul and physical body. Following Jesus's example, ordinary people interpreted the New Testament literally—freely casting out evil spirits and healing the sick as a normal part of their spiritual lives.

Today, deliverance ministry is being resurrected as the spirit of God is at work raising up a company of believers who are called to boldly proclaim the truth—many of whom are once again seeking to fulfill this *God-given mandate* (Matthew 10:8). We are living in an hour when we must no longer ignore the subject of deliverance, but rather embrace this ministry as one body in Christ. All too few are finding the freedom that only Jesus Christ can give, as they seek to understand the full work of the cross—with its provision not only for the forgiveness of our sins, but for healing, divine health, and deliverance as well. It's time that we reconsider the meaning of the *full gospel* and the importance of deliverance ministry for the sake of the many who are suffering in our midst.

We must be faithful to preach the whole council of God (Acts 20:26, 27) for we know we will be held accountable. It is a fact that many in the church have failed to preach and teach what the Word of God says about healing and deliverance. Therefore, we see God's people being destroyed for the lack of this knowledge (Hosea 4:6).

Though deliverance ministry continues to be opposed, today it is becoming more widely accepted—as many tormented souls seek the help that they need so desperately. God is at work setting His people free as we see a release when deliverance prayer is ministered effectively. Nevertheless, we must exercise much caution and discernment in order to maintain balance—always looking to the Holy Spirit for divine wisdom in every situation we may encounter.

> *Ask, and it will be given to you; seek, and you will find; knock, and it will be opened to you.*
>
> *Matthew 7:7*

Prologue

*Sanctify them through thy truth:
thy word is truth.*

John 17:17

Do you need a miracle? Is there something in your life that you cannot seem to gain the victory over? Maybe you've tried everything you know to do but have found no relief. I believe God has a miracle for you today. I believe what He's done for many others, He will do for you. Know that there is nothing impossible with God for those who will believe (Luke 1:37). As we learn the truth together, and act upon that truth, we can and will be *miraculously set free.*

Though there are a number of wonderful resources on this subject, my purpose in this writing is not only to briefly consider the facts concerning deliverance ministry, but more importantly to provide for you a simple *hands-on guide* that will show you step by step how you can experience freedom from that which may be holding you captive.

Many today are struggling with various kinds of problems, but be assured that as we undertake careful study (2 Timothy 2:15), you or someone you care deeply about can find the truth you've been looking for—that can bring you the freedom you desire.

I have *good news* for you. Every provision for personal deliverance has been made for you (Philippians 4:19) so that you can be set free. Is there something that has taken a toll on you mentally, emotionally, physically, or even spiritually? Whatever your need, know that God wants to set you free in every area of your life.

Divine Revelation

We will learn the true source behind some of the things that you may be struggling with. It's time that the truth be told through God-given revelations from the Word of God, as the Holy Spirit brings His truth into our hearts. We must know that this revelation is not understood in its definition only, but it must also be experienced in our everyday lives. In the *four gospels* of the New Testament, we see that Jesus always connected the truth with an experience.

What do we mean by "divine revelation"? Revelation is the knowledge of God's Word which is suddenly revealed to your spirit by the Holy Spirit without prior knowledge (John 16:13). Today, God is restoring biblical truth through new revelations, which have not always been known or taught throughout the history of the church. Tragically, the truth has been replaced with much that is often untrue. However, be reassured that God wants each of us to prosper in all things and be blessed with divine health and freedom from every form of bondage (3 John 2).

New Voices

Today, many voices are being raised up by the Holy Spirit, "The spirit of truth who will guide us into all truth" (John 16:13), for we are told, "If you know the truth, that truth will set you free" (John 8:32). We must begin with the facts and then go beyond mere intellectualism and experience the truth for ourselves.

The Greek word "to know" means to have an *experience*, or to experience in our hearts that which cannot be defined with the mind alone. It is my heart's desire that through this writing, you will not only hear the truth about deliverance, but that you will begin to experience that truth for yourself as a way of life. I want to take you through the "process of self-deliverance" so that you can experience the release that you may have been desperately seeking for some time.

You may be thinking at this point, "What really is the truth, and can I really know the truth?" According to the *American Heritage Dictionary*, truth is defined as a statement proven to be or accepted as true with all sincerity and integrity. It is the quality of being in one accord with the *facts*. It is a comprehensive term that in all its nuances implies accuracy and honesty.

What is the Truth?

It is important that we settle in our minds and hearts once and for all whether the Word of God, which we refer to as the Bible, really is indeed the truth. Jesus who claimed to be the Son of God stated in (John 8:40) that "no prophecy of the Scriptures is of any private interpretation, but that it came not in old time by the will of man: but holy men of God spake as they were moved by the Holy Spirit." Therefore, we must come by faith with a *teachable spirit*, and when we do, the Spirit of God will confirm in our spirit that this book we call the Word of God is indeed just that—the truth.

It is absolutely necessary that you believe without a doubt—because every work of God, and in this case the miracle of deliverance, must be received again by faith in God's Word. (James 1:7) says we should not expect to receive anything from God without faith. Know that God has given to each one of us *"a measure of faith"* (Romans 12:3) so that you already have all the faith you need to believe and receive your miracle of deliverance.

Here's the Plan

We are going to learn more about deliverance, the deliverance process and what *steps* we need to take in order to experience personal deliverance on a regular basis. We will also discuss *root causes* and possible *open doors* which we may have allowed that can lead to various kinds of torment. You will learn everything you need to know in order to be set free and stay free as a way of life. If you will "do your part" and persevere until you experience the freedom you need, deliverance is yours to claim as a child of God. So as we continue, let's pray the following prayer *out loud* together!

Pray: Lord Jesus, I seek to know the truth so I ask you to confirm Your Word in my life (Mark 16:20). By Your Holy Spirit, I want to receive the revelation I need in order to experience freedom from the things that have held me captive. In Your name, I pray. Amen.

When he, the Spirit of truth is come, he will guide you into all truth: for he shall not speak of himself; but whatsoever he shall hear, that shall he speak: and he will show you things to come.

John 16:13

Introduction

*Think soberly, as God has dealt to
each one a measure of faith.*

Romans 12:3

It seems today even among Christians, that very little is known about deliverance ministry. Most are not aware that there may just be something or someone behind the various trials that we all experience during the course of our lifetime. This being the case, we must not undertake this study lightly, nor should we hastily enter into the process of deliverance without first carefully preparing ourselves with the facts. Come with an open mind and a teachable spirit—laying aside perhaps preconceived ideas and even lifelong prejudices.

I ask that the God of our Lord Jesus Christ would give to us the spirit of wisdom, revelation, and eyes and ears of understanding so that we may know our full inheritance in Him (Ephesians 1:17, 18). It is very important that the Holy Spirit guide us into all truth as we purpose in our hearts to look to Him for the needed revelation we must have revealed to our spirit.

It is also very important that you know that you are a *child of God*, and that you have been spiritually reborn or *born again* through the "new birth experience" (John 3:3). Only those who truly know Jesus Christ as Savior and Lord have been given the power and authority over all the power of the enemy (Luke 10:19). Therefore, we must carefully determine whether we have had such an encounter. Can you truly say, "I know whom I have believed, and I am persuaded that He (Jesus) is able to keep that which I have committed unto him" (2 Timothy 1:12)?

> *Stop*! Let's take a moment to meditate upon our relationship with Christ. If you are not sure that heaven is your home and that your name is written in the *Lamb's Book of Life* (Revelation 3:5), I invite you to pray with heartfelt faith the following prayer *out loud.*

Pray: Lord Jesus, I repent of my sins, and I believe that you died on the cross for me. I invite you to come into my heart and life and save me now. I make you my Lord and Savior today. Amen.

Importance of Review

During our study, it will be necessary to review from time to time important truths. The fact is that we often have to hear something many times before we can receive its revelation down in our spirit. This is the reason you will be asked to "stop and meditate" in order to fully understand what you are reading.

If you are serious about being set free, this book should not be regarded as a "quick read-through." It should be viewed as a *manual* that you will refer back to many times in the days to come as you put into practice what you need to do to achieve total deliverance.

We will also be declaring a "statement of faith" at the end of each chapter for we are told when we "decree a thing" every word will be established for us (Job 22:28).

Confession of Faith

Lord Jesus, I want to know the truth so I can be set free from the things that hold me captive. Help me grasp what You want me to learn as I wait upon You and meditate upon Your Word. I am trusting you to deliver me out of all my troubles (Psalm 34:17). In Your name, I pray. Amen.

What I tell you in darkness, that speak ye in the light: and what ye hear in the ear, that preach ye upon the housetops.

Matthew 10:27

We are now ready to begin to search the Scriptures together for "the truth that will set you free" (John 8:32) from everything that may be holding you in some form of bondage.

Chapter 1

Jesus's Deliverance Ministry

The Spirit of the Lord is upon me, because he hath anointed me to preach deliverance to the captives, and recovering of sight to the blind, and to set at liberty them that are bruised.

Luke 4:18

The Compassion of Jesus Christ

Jesus Christ came to set captives free!

After considering a number of scriptures from the New Testament of the Bible, we see that Jesus not only believed in deliverance, but that He ministered deliverance openly and often. Jesus said that He came to earth to set captives free, and He *commissioned* His followers to do the same. It is clear that Jesus Christ, who declared Himself to be the Son of God (John 10:36) took deliverance ministry seriously.

It is a fact, that at least one-third of Jesus's ministry involved casting out demons. In the above verse of scripture, Jesus literally preached deliverance to those who were held captive, as He ministered the *good news* of the gospel from town to town. With great compassion, He healed and set free all who came to Him who were in desperate need of a miracle, and He is still doing the same today.

Very early in His ministry among the people, Jesus clearly announced the purpose of His Spirit-anointed ministry, which included not only preaching the gospel to the destitute and afflicted, but also healing those who were bruised and oppressed. He declared that His Father in heaven had sent Him to *proclaim freedom* for the prisoners (Luke 4:18), and to open spiritual eyes of those blinded by the world and Satan. This truth is so important if we are to affectively fulfill our divine purpose and destiny in this life—which is the reason for which we were born.

Let the Truth Be Told

Until the truth is "shouted from the housetops" (Matthew 10:27), multitudes of suffering people in our churches and communities will not receive the help they need. It's time that *evil be confronted* and denial and deception be exposed. Delivering people from evil spirits, forgiving sins, and healing the sick are essential to

Jesus went about healing all who were oppressed by the devil!

the gospel—for "God anointed Jesus of Nazareth with the Holy Ghost and with power: who went about doing good, and healing all that were oppressed of the devil; for God was with him" (Acts 10:38).

(Ephesians 6:12) says, "We do not wrestle against flesh and blood, but against principalities, against powers, against the rulers of the darkness of this age, and against spiritual wickedness in heavenly places." Only as we free the oppressed and heal all who are suffering with sickness and disease, will we be able to say that the kingdom of God is at hand, and the kingdom of Satan is being destroyed.

It is clear that Jesus's foremost concern in His ministry was to destroy the works of the devil—seen in various encounters in which Jesus strongly opposed the kingdom of darkness. Yes, it was for this purpose that He had come into the world (1 John 3:8).

One of Jesus's first acts in His ministry was to enter into direct conflict with the demonic. When Jesus came in contact with demonic spirits, He boldly *cast them out* of people's lives— often setting them free from a lifetime of great misery and torment (Matthew 8:28–34).

> *Stop*! Taking time-out to meditate upon what you read will enable you to receive the revelation you need from the Holy Spirit.

Encounters with Demons

Let's now take a look at several passages of Scripture, as reported by Jesus's disciples in the four gospels of the New Testament. These confirm the *validity* of deliverance ministry. May they stir our hearts with the same passion and compassion that Jesus displayed wherever He went—always remembering "whom the son sets free is free indeed" (John 8:36).

With authority He commanded unclean spirits!

Jesus Drives Out an Evil Spirit

We read in (Luke 4:33–37) at the synagogue of Capernaum, about a man who had many demons who cried out, "Let us alone, what have we to do with thee; thou Jesus Christ of Nazareth, art thou come to destroy us? I know thee who thou art; the Holy One of God."

"And Jesus rebuked him, saying, 'Hold thy peace and come out of him.' And when the devil had thrown him in the midst, he came out of him, and hurt him not. Then all the people were all amazed and spoke among themselves, saying, 'What a word this is! For with authority and power He commands the unclean spirits, and they come out'. And the report about Him went out into every place in the surrounding region."

A Demon-Possessed Man Healed

We read in the gospel of (Luke 8:26–37) that a certain man lived in the tombs who had demons for a long time. When he saw Jesus, he cried out with a loud voice, "What have I to do with You, Jesus, Son of the Most High God? I beg You, do not torment me! For He had commanded the unclean spirit to come out of the man. For it had often seized him, and he was kept under guard, bound with chains and shackles; and he broke the bonds and was driven by the demon into the wilderness."

Demons do not want to be cast into the abyss!

Jesus went about healing all who were oppressed by the devil!

Jesus asked him saying, "What is your name? Legion, because many demons had entered him. And they begged Him that He would not command them to go out into the abyss. Now a herd of many swine was feeding there on the mountain. So they begged Him that He would permit them to enter them. And He permitted them. Then the demons went out of the man and entered the swine, and the herd ran violently down the steep place into the lake and drowned."

"When those who fed them saw what had happened, they fled and told it in the city and in the country. Then they went out to see what had happened, and came to Jesus, and found the man from whom the demons had departed, sitting at the feet of Jesus, clothed and in his right mind."

A Boy with an Evil Spirit

Let's consider now the cry of a father's heart for his son who was severely oppressed by a demon in (Luke 9:37– 42). "Suddenly a man cried out saying, 'Teacher, I implore You, look on my son, for he is my only child. And behold, a spirit seizes him, and he suddenly cries out; it convulses him so that he foams at the mouth; and it departs from him with great difficulty, bruising him. So I implored Your disciples to cast it out, but they could not'. 'Bring your son here.' And as he was still coming, the demon threw him down and convulsed him. Then Jesus rebuked the unclean spirit, healed the child, and gave him back to his father."

A Woman with a Spirit of Infirmity

"Now Jesus was teaching in one of the synagogues on the Sabbath. And, behold, there was a woman which had a spirit of infirmity eighteen years, and was bowed together, and could in no wise lift up herself. And when Jesus saw her, he called her to him, and said unto her, 'Woman, thou art loosed from thine infirmity.' And he laid his hands on her: and immediately she was made straight, and glorified God."

"Jesus declared, 'Ought not this woman, being a daughter of Abraham, whom Satan hath bound, lo, these eighteen years, be loosed from this bond on the Sabbath day?' And all the people rejoiced for all the glorious things that were done by him" (Luke 13:11–16).

Other Accounts

Listed below you will find several additional passages of Scripture that you may want to consider for further study.

The people rejoiced to see many captives set free!

1. Peter's mother-in-law was delivered of a spirit of fever (Luke 4:38, 39).
2. Jesus delivered a man who could not speak because of a dumb spirit (Matthew 9:32).
3. A man who was possessed was delivered from

a spirit of blindness and a dumb spirit (Matthew 12:22).
4. A woman's daughter was delivered who had been demonized because of generational curses (Matthew 15:23–28).

Our Response

What can we observe from the above encounters? Note once again that the people were certainly desperate and in need of divine intervention, and that Jesus *responded immediately* with great compassion to their needs in every situation— which He attributed to Satan and the presence of demons or unclean spirits. He clearly made known to the people the source of their desperate condition.

Authority and power were demonstrated in the midst of the people, and they were amazed to see demon spirits flee. At the words of Jesus, they had no choice but to surrender their will and obey. Their greatest fear seemed to be in being sent to the "abyss", which is defined as a bottomless gulf or pit extending below the earth.

Jesus will respond immediately to your need!

Every Provision

Today, you too may be in a situation where there seems to be no hope and you wonder, "Can God really deliver me out of all my troubles" (Psalm 34:17)? You may be struggling with an addiction, a physical sickness, or disease where there is no cure, or something that continues to torment you in the depths of your soul.

It is time that we come to understand what may be causing these problems in our lives. The *good news* is that Jesus has made every provision for us, and regardless of our need, there is nothing that God cannot do. Absolutely nothing (Luke 1:37)! We also know that Jesus is "no respecter of persons" (Romans 2:11). So as we continue, let faith arise in your heart. Expect God to miraculously set you free as you *hear and act upon* the revelations you need to receive—deep down in your spirit from the Word of God. As we come together in agreement (Matthew 18:19), I expect whatever you need to manifest in your life. Remember, Jesus is "a very present help in time of trouble" (Psalm 46:1). We see consistently in the Scriptures that He never turned anyone away for a later time.

Healed of Depression

Before leaving this chapter, I'd like to include here a word concerning my own personal experience as I now engage in deliverance regularly. For most of my life, perhaps like you, I did not know the *true source* of many of my own struggles. As far back as I can remember, I lived with on-going depression. Though I did not seek help until I was an adult, through the study of deliverance ministry, I have since learned that the root cause for much emotional suffering was a number of unclean spirits that I had literally allowed to torment me. Depression was the result of a *generational curse* passed down to me through my ancestors. We will be talking about these curses in a later chapter.

Today, when negative emotions oppress or unacceptable circumstances seek to trouble me and others, with the authority God has given me, I now firmly rebuke and cast out these demonic spirits as I become aware of them. The wonderful thing is that when we do what Jesus has told us to do, freedom and a sense of release are ours to enjoy.

It is this truth on personal deliverance that I wish to share with you through this writing so that you too can live a life free from all torment and oppression. Yes, as long as Satan is free to seek to devour all of mankind (1 Peter 5:8), the battle will continue. However, when we *resist the devil* and all who are a part of his kingdom as we draw near to God, he will flee from us (James 4:7).

So be encouraged! The deliverance you need is "yours for the taking" as a child of God. Read on as we learn the truth together which will set you free. It's time that we rise up with boldness of spirit and say "Enough is enough!"

> *Stop!* Always take a moment to carefully review
> before going on to the next chapter!

Chapter Review!

1. Jesus declared that He was sent by God His Father to set free those who were bound by the devil.
2. His heart of compassion reached out to all the people as He ministered deliverance wherever He went.
3. What He continues to do around the world today, He will do for you.
4. Jesus boldly cast out demons and every believer is called to do the same.

Confession of Faith

Before going on to the next chapter, let's agree (Matthew 18:19) as we make a confession of our faith together *out loud*. Remember that according to (Mark 11:23, 24), when you pray and do not doubt in your heart, whatever you say you shall have.

> *Heavenly Father, I am so grateful for your heart of compassion toward all who suffer and are in pain. Thank you for sending your son Jesus so that I can be set free from all my troubles. I believe what You are doing for others You will do for me. Help me to receive from Your Holy Spirit the revelation that I need, today. In Jesus's name, I pray. Amen.*
>
> *Jesus Christ is the same yesterday, today, and forever.*
>
> Hebrews 13:8

Now, having established the significance of Jesus's deliverance ministry, in the next chapter, let's consider the reality of demonic activity in the world in which we live.

Chapter 2

Do Demons Really Exist?

In that same hour he cured many of their infirmities and plagues, and of evil spirits;

Luke 7:21

The Early Church

We see from the gospels of the New Testament of the Bible that during the first century, few seemed to question the existence of unclean spirits. Encounters with the demonic were common, and there were many who were clearly in need of deliverance. Early Christians were very much aware of the presence of demonic spirits, and they actively sought to exercise discernment— "having their senses exercised to discern both good and evil" (Hebrews 5:14) as they cast out demons in fulfillment of the "great commission" (Mark 16:17).

Awareness of demons was common!

Today, Christians around the world from all walks of life are becoming more and more aware of deliverance ministry and the reality of demonic activity—even though much of the body of Christ does not minister deliverance as part of the work of the local church. Nevertheless, there is an awakening taking place because of the suffering that is so prevalent among God's people.

In the Beginning

As we continue our study on deliverance, we need to understand some facts about the devil, his demons, their origin, and how the kingdom of darkness operates. Jesus referred to the devil as the "ruler or prince of this world" (John 12:31), and in (Ephesians 2:2) he is called "the ruler of the power of the air, the spirit that is now at work among those who are disobedient." As a created being, he has been allowed to have power for a season, but that power is subject to the sovereignty of God.

Satan is behind all that is evil in the world today!

Satan and one-third of the angels were cast down to the earth!

The Bible tells us that God created all things including many spirit beings or angels. (Hebrews 1:14) says many angels are sent as ministering spirits to serve those who will inherit salvation—through faith in Jesus Christ. However, (Ephesians 6:12) speaks of evil spirits or *fallen angels* who war against all of mankind. You may be wondering, "What happened that brought about this struggle between good and evil?"

(Isaiah 14:12–15) tells us that Lucifer, also known as Satan or the devil, rebelled in heaven, and with one-third of all the angels who followed him, they were cast down to the earth. The spirits of these beings are now the demons whose final destination is the *lake of fire* (Revelation 20:10). However, for the time being, they look for bodies to inhabit in order to manifest themselves.

"How art thou fallen from heaven, O Lucifer, son of the morning! How art thou cut down to the ground, which didst weaken the nations! For thou hast said in thine heart, I will ascend into heaven, I will exalt my throne above the stars of God: I will sit also upon the mount of the congregation, in the sides of the north: I will ascend above the heights of the clouds; I will be like the most High. Yet thou shalt be brought down to hell, to the sides of the pit" (Isaiah 14:12–15).

According to Scripture, Satan fell because of pride. He was most likely the highest of all the angels—the most beautiful of all God's creation, but he was not content in his position.

For the present time, two powerful kingdoms operate in this world in which we live—the kingdom of God and the kingdom of Satan. Jesus described this situation as a clash between two spiritual kingdoms which He said is why He came into this world—to set captives free and to liberate those enslaved by demonic powers.

John Avincini in his book *Stolen Property Returned* has made the following statement:

"If there is a key thought in this book, it has to be this: The devil is the mastermind behind every evil act that takes place on this earth. The Bible abounds with evidence that he and his demons are the villains behind all the trouble that we see in the world today. Whether it be sickness, disappointment, robbery, or what have you, the source of the problem is the same. It is the devil."

Stop! Let's thoroughly meditate for a moment here on the above!

What is a Demon?

According to well-known author Frank Hammond, demons are *spirit beings* with evil personalities. Demons are tormentors. They are enemies of God and man. Their objectives are to tempt, deceive, accuse, condemn, pressure, defile, resist, oppose, control, steal, afflict, kill, and destroy. Demons enter through open doors caused by sin. They like to take full advantage of *times of weakness* in our lives where and whenever possible, and we have found that many have entered during childhood, and even from a mother's womb.

Demons possess knowledge, they have a will and emotions, and they are not things. Demons are spirit beings who have personalities and intelligence. As members of Satan's kingdom, they are evil and malicious and under Satan's authority. They are named according to their manifestations such as fear, anger, and unbelief.

Demons seek to inhabit a body which they call their house!

They are also frequently referred to as "unclean spirits". Demons can and do live in the bodies of human beings—influencing men, women, and children to do evil.

The Bible makes it clear that these evil beings dwell in the realm of the spirit and are too many to count. They seek a body to inhabit where they have been given *legal right* to do so. They can freely bring harm to anyone when we are not aware of their presence and agenda. They often gather in groups which are identified as thrones, powers (Colossians 1:16), and authorities (1 Peter 3:22). (See Section: "Demon Groupings")

What Do Demons Do?

Demons are at work today just as they have always been. We know that demons can cause physical illness in the human body, although some believe that not all sickness is caused by evil spirits. We are told that they will be especially active in the last days of this age (2 Timothy 3:1) promoting the occult, immorality, violence, and every form of cruelty.

They actively assault the integrity of God's Word, every believer in Christ, and they deny the work of the cross which purchased the forgiveness of our sin, healing, divine health, and our deliverance, safety, and protection. However, "hell" is the place of eternal torment that has been prepared by God for the devil and his demons (2 Peter 2:4).

Satan is expert in turning people away from the truth!

The Bible clearly teaches that there will come in the "last days", a departure from the faith, and surely that day is upon us. The devil and his armies of evil spirits bring doctrines, often unknowingly, into the church that have no biblical foundation. They are expert in the art of seducing and turning aside people from the truth. They come to people in times of doubt and unbelief, some deep sorrow, or some *spiritual failure*. They also seek to introduce seeds of false teaching, which in time can shipwreck one's faith (1 Timothy 1:19).

"Now the Spirit speaketh expressly, that in the latter times some shall depart from the faith, giving heed to seducing spirits, and doctrines of devils" (1 Timothy 4:1).

> *Stop!* Let's take some time here to review the facts about demons!

People Are Not Our Problem

I have found great comfort in knowing who and what is really behind the many trials we all face throughout our lifetime. When a person attacks you in some way, view this not as a human attack but a spiritual one—where demon spirits have created *strongholds* in their life and mind. It's important that we seek discernment into what motivates a person's behavior. We must look beyond the person and see what's really going on in and through that person. People are not our problem. It's the demons that use them to harass us in whatever way they can.

We also need to realize that unless we have been delivered and continue to be delivered, demon spirits can use any one of us to bring great harm to others—spirits of gossip, anger, accusation, condemnation, criticism, rejection, rebellion, murder, incest, lies, deception, and many other spirits that seek to bring torment—just to name a few.

Demons use people to hurt other people!

You will find at the end of the book an extensive *list of demonic spirits*—many of which we may struggle with on a daily basis. When we begin to recognize the source of many of our problems and learn what we must do to confront them, much oppression of the devil can be stopped. Again, (James 4:7) reminds us that as we draw near to God and resist the devil, he will flee from us.

(Ephesians 6:11–13) also commands that we "Put on the whole armor of God, that ye may be able to stand against the wiles (or schemes) of the devil. For we wrestle not against flesh and blood, (people) but against principalities, against powers, against the rulers of the darkness of this world, and against spiritual wickedness in high places."

Put on the whole armor of God and keep it on!

Yes, demons are real and they do exist. As I previously shared, I have been and continue to be delivered from much oppression on a daily basis. No, it's not easy! It's a battle we must face every single day as long as we dwell upon the earth. We must never forget that Satan is determined to destroy all of our lives if allowed.

Acknowledging this truth is the first step we must take if we are to walk in the freedom that is ours in Christ. Therefore, if there is any question in your mind, I pray that the Holy Spirit will impart to your spirit this revelation as only He can. This is my earnest prayer for you!

Recognize that there is a battle going on with the devil and his kingdom every day!

Stop! Let's meditate on this truth,
lest we fall into deception and unbelief.

Chapter Review!

1. There are two powerful kingdoms operating in our world today; the kingdom of Satan and the kingdom of God.
2. Unlike the early church, many believers today are unaware that they have a very real enemy they must resist.
3. Due to a lack of clear teaching and sound doctrine, few understand or even practice personal deliverance.
4. Satan and his demons are real, and there is great evidence that they are behind all the troubles that we see taking place in our world today.
5. Our battle is not with mankind, but with spirit beings that use people to accomplish their evil deeds.

Confession of Faith

Let's make the following confession of faith *out loud* together.

> Lord Jesus, thank you for sharing the truth from Your Word concerning the reality of Satan and his kingdom. You said when I know the truth, the truth will set me free. Teach me all that I need to know so that I will not fall prey to Satan's devices. Open my eyes that I may see clearly every deception of the enemy, and continue to prepare me to walk in the victory that You purchased for me through the cross of Calvary. In Your name, I pray. Amen.

And let us not be weary in well doing: for in due season we shall reap, if we faint not.

Galatians 6:9

In the next chapter, you will learn much more about deliverance, as we continue to seek the whole truth and nothing but the truth together. Remember, God has given every believer the mind of Christ (1 Corinthians 2:16), divine wisdom from above (Ephesians 1:17), and spiritual discernment so that you can be gloriously set free (Philippians 1:9).

Chapter 3

What is Deliverance?

And these signs shall follow them that believe; In my name shall they cast out devils;

Mark 16:17

Casting Out Demons

The process of expelling demons is called "deliverance". When deliverance is needed, the biblical method of deliverance is to cast out demons by commanding them to go in the *name of Jesus*. It is important to know that they cannot be counseled out or coaxed out. Wherever they are present, they must literally be *forced out*.

Demons are the reason for many of your problems!

Deliverance is also defined as "a rescue from bondage or danger." The generally agreed-upon definition of deliverance ministry refers to the activity of cleansing a person of demons or unclean spirits in order to address problems manifesting in their life. Deliverance ministry focuses on casting out demons in an attempt to set free those who are being tormented and oppressed.

Keeping in mind that Christ's commission to the church clearly included the practice of casting out demons (Mark 16:17), please note that the terms unclean spirit, evil spirit, and devils or demons are used interchangeably in the gospels of the New Testament. These words were used to describe beings having varying degrees of supernatural power. We will use these terms when referring to the enemy and his kingdom throughout this writing.

Deliverance ministry is setting many free today!

Some have asked, "What happens to the demons that are cast out?" (Matthew 12:43) says, "When the unclean spirit is gone out of a man, he walketh through dry places seeking rest and findeth none." Therefore, we might conclude that a demon is restless outside of a human body.

Ready For Battle

We honestly need to find out what part deliverance can and should play in each of our lives and those around us, and then seek to receive whatever benefit possible. Unfortunately, the prospect of having demons has prevented all too many from seeking the help that they need. Though we cannot put all the blame on Satan and his demons for our problems, we are finding out that we can blame them for much more than we *once thought possible.*

Strongly resist every work of the enemy!

Though many have not yet learned that demons are responsible for many of their troubles—when we do, we should seriously seek getting rid of them as quickly as possible. Issues that may not have been resolved through prayer and fasting, are now being solved through deliverance ministry.

Nowhere in the Word of God does it suggest that God will do anything about demonic activity, for He's done all He's going to do for the time being through Christ's sacrifice on the cross. Every believer has to do something about the devil for themselves. As with divine healing, we have an important *part to play* in living free of sickness and various bondages through-out our lifetime. We must be prepared to resist Satan daily.

This is why we are told to put on the armor of God in (Ephesians 6:10–12)—a truth that bears repeating. The apostle Paul said when writing to the church at Ephesus,

Jesus has already done all that He is going to do!

"Be strong in the Lord, and in the power of his might. Put on the whole armor of God that ye may be able to stand against the wiles of the devil. For we wrestle not against flesh and blood, but against principalities, against powers, against the rulers of the darkness of this world, and against spiritual wickedness in high places."

> *Stop!* Meditate on the reality of Satan's kingdom in your life and the world!

Our Mandate

As previously shared, I was not taught the truth about the source of many of my problems—though it has been many years since I was *born again* through faith in Jesus Christ. This is tragic and all too often the norm and not the exception for most Christians. This is why it is the mandate of *Waves of Glory Miracle Ministries* to proclaim the "gospel truth" about healing and deliverance around the world.

Boldly take back what's been stolen from you!

Satan is a very real enemy who seeks to steal, kill, and destroy everything we hold dear. So we must learn to stand against him and his kingdom if we are to walk in the abundant life that Jesus came to give us (John 10:10). When we do, life is so much better. Let's listen once again to what John Avancini has to say about this in his book *Stolen Property Returned*.

"It is time for you to serve notice on the devil. He has robbed you long enough. Don't allow him to diminish your quality of life a day longer. You can stop him now! It's time for you to take a stand! The devil is a defeated foe! The power he once had is over forever. Jesus was sent to destroy all of his works and He did—overcoming sin, sickness, death, and the devil for all mankind.

Isn't it time that we all lay hold of this truth? It's time that we reclaim everything that's been stolen from us. The devil has ruled over the affairs of mankind for far too long. It's time that we realize that he has no power—compared to the power God has given to every believer. The devil has no power over us except what you and I give him (1 John 5:4). Enough is enough!"

Know that our ministry is dedicated to this end. "Let the truth be told! Shout it from the rooftops!" The Lord spoke these words to me so clearly in 2011 during a time of prayer and fasting! It's time that every Christian stand united in doing everything possible to stop Satan from achieving his goals. Know that we are standing with other ministries in every way possible—through seminars, conferences, radio ministry, various forms of media, and our Miracle Healing Prayer Center now located in Western New York. Healing deliverance ministry are available with classes to equip you to walk in the miraculous where miracles are a normal part of everyday life. We covet your prayers and support!

Stop! Meditate on the reality of our adversary
and what we must do to confront him!

Chapter Review!

1. Deliverance is achieved by casting out demons in the name of Jesus.
2. There is nothing more for Jesus to do. The work of the cross is complete.
3. Satan is behind many of our problems and much of our suffering.
4. We must put on and keep on God's armor as we stand against the devil and his demons.
5. When you resist the enemy he will flee from you.

Confession of Faith

Let's make the following confession of faith *out loud* together.

Heavenly Father, I am so grateful that You have provided deliverance for me and my loved ones from Satan's attacks. Thank you for the full-set of armor you have provided for me and the strength to use it. I believe that as I resist the devil he will flee from me. I give the devil no place in my life. In Jesus's name, I pray. Amen.

And lead us not into temptation but deliver us from evil.

Matthew 6:13

As we continue, let's discuss in greater detail the truth concerning *Satan's agenda* in the life of every believer. Satan is no respecter of persons. He seeks to steal, kill, and destroy every person on the planet—especially those who profess faith in Jesus Christ.

Chapter 4

Can a Christian Have a Demon?

*For His merciful kindness is great toward us,
And the truth of the Lord endures forever.*

Psalm 117:2

Nothing but the Truth

This is an important question that many have asked. Based upon what we have already discussed about deliverance, we can draw no other conclusion. Even though many dispute this truth for themselves and many pastors for their congregations, believers have and are experiencing freedom when demons are cast out.

Satan's biggest lie is that he is not real and that you cannot have a demon!

It is a fact that more and more of the body of Christ and the Church as we know it today are embracing this truth as never before. This awakening is long overdue.

Again, any confusion is the result of the lack of clear teaching on this subject, and satan's attempt to keep the truth from being known for hundreds of years—the truth concerning the presence of demonic activity and our need to *practice personal deliverance* on a daily basis. The New Testament makes no distinction between believers and nonbelievers in regard to casting out demons. Therefore, the obvious conclusion is that everyone is being tragically affected by Satan and his demonic kingdom.

Well-known author Don Dickerman has written the following concerning Christians and demons as a result of working with inmates in prison ministry.

More are embracing the truth that all have been affected by demons!

"Inmates would seek me out, tell me they had demons, and ask me to help them. These were always believers, and I had always been taught that Christians could not have demons. I now believe this is the biggest lie that Satan has perpetrated on the body of Christ. The deception is so great that most believers will not even consider that they may be demonically oppressed. Christians can and often do have demons both in their soul and physical bodies—working great oppression in their lives."

You can have demons in your body and soul!

Seek Divine Wisdom

Wisdom suggests that what we are taught must always be subject to what we have experienced. I'm sure we all agree that knowing is always better than believing. You can believe that you don't have a demon. You can believe that a Christian cannot be *demonized*, but that does not change the facts. Like this author, I too know that it does happen, because as I have already stated, I have been greatly relieved of much torment and know of many others who have as well.

Knowing what I now know has compelled me to join a growing number of voices who are proclaiming this truth as the Holy Spirit directs—when and wherever possible through *Waves of Glory Miracle Ministries*. It is long overdue that Satan and the kingdom of darkness be exposed. The cry of my heart is that all would come to the knowledge of the truth, and experience the freedom that is available in Christ—no longer bound by the lies of the enemy (1 Timothy 2:4).

You may be like many others who question deliverance. Nevertheless, you must settle this issue in your heart and mind once and for all. Believers can and often do have demon spirits dwelling in them, on them and around them. The myth that this cannot be has kept the church in bondage. The Word of God declares, "Where there is no *vision* (revelation), the people perish" (Proverb 29:18), and "My people are destroyed for lack of knowledge" (Hosea 4:6).

We might say that the lack of the truth is willful ignorance. The fact is that the presence of the Holy Spirit does not prevent evil spirits from dwelling in a believer's body or soul. You can know God's Word, teach and preach that Word and even memorize that Word, and still have demons. Again, believing that Christians cannot have demons is a dangerous and widely held view, but nevertheless, a *false misconception*. Let me explain more fully how this can possibly be true.

Stop! Take time to pray and meditate
as needed before reading on.

Our Spirit Reborn

We must understand that when a person is "born again" spiritually through faith in Jesus Christ (John 3:3), that individual is now able to communicate with God the Father, Jesus His son, and God's Holy Spirit. Previous to that we were separated from God by our sin.

(Ephesians 2:1) says, "You hath he (Holy Spirit) quickened, who were dead in trespasses and sins; Wherein in time past ye walked according to the course of this world, according to the prince of the power of the air, (Satan) the spirit that now worketh in the children of disobedience: Among whom also we all had our

As a Christian Satan has no access to your spirit!

conversation in times past in the lusts of our flesh fulfilling the desires of the flesh and of the mind; and were by nature the children of wrath, even as others. But God, who is rich in mercy, for his great love wherewith he loved us, even when we were dead in sins, hath quickened us together with Christ."

With this life-changing experience, our spirit is renewed and our sins are forgiven or "blotted out" (Acts 3:19). Therefore, Satan does not have access to our spirit because we have been sealed by the Holy Spirit (Ephesians 1:13). However, it is important to note here again, that Satan and his demons can touch our souls and bodies through open doors caused by our own sin (Psalm 103:3), the sins of our ancestors (Exodus 20:5) or the sins of those who have sinned against us (Luke 15:21). The lack of this understanding is why there is so much misunderstanding among God's people.

Revelation or Human Logic

Though it may seem logical that a demon cannot indwell the body of a Christian at the same time as the Holy Spirit—all logic is not necessarily the truth. Demon spirits can invade human bodies, and it is their objective to do so—in order to gain greater control over a person's life.

Demons seek to indwell every human body even from birth!

Demons consider the body of a person to be their house (Matthew 12:44). When demons indwell a person, it is said that they have evil or unclean spirits. Therefore, to be free from all torment, they must be confronted and cast out. As shared previously, we saw Jesus doing this during His earthly ministry on many occasions.

Norvel Hayes in his book, *How To Cast Out Demons* states clearly:

"Casting out devils brings healing to the *inner man*." Jesus has taught that every human being is going to be affected. We must get the devils out and get them filled with God. You may not even know what's wrong with you. You need to come to Jesus and be set free by God's power. And you can be set free."

Norvel goes on to say, "It doesn't make any difference what other people think. It's what God's Word says that matters. Jesus said to cast out devils in His name if you are a believer" (Mark 16:17). Again, we must understand that the devil hates the human race (Genesis 3:15).

Believe what God says in His Word and not what people think!

Nevertheless, Jesus has taught us how to take authority over Satan and his kingdom."

Frank Hammond in his book *Demons and Deliverance: Life of Jesus*, has also shared how we can understand the demonization of a Christian. He states:

"The question is 'Can property owned by one person be trespassed upon by another person'? A trespasser can come upon that property, but he can also be put off the property. This is what takes place when a demon indwells a Christian. Therefore, when the evil spirit is commanded to go by that person or another Christian, the evil spirit has no choice but to obey."

These truths can only be received through divine revelation!

Stop! Spend time here and meditate on this important truth.

Not Your Spirit

We cannot overemphasize the important distinction that must be made if we are to understand the presence of a demon in the life of a believer. Mankind was created as a three-part being. The first commandment makes the distinction between our body, soul, and spirit very clear. (Mark 12:30) states that we are to love the Lord our God with all our heart which is our spirit, with all our soul, and with all our strength— referring to our physical body.

Once again, understand that only the spirit is renewed through the "new birth" experience and not our body or soul.

Only our spirit becomes a new creation when old things pass away and all things become new (2 Corinthians 5:17). Therefore, it is possible for our physical bodies and souls to be affected by Satan and his kingdom of demons, but not our spirit.

Legal Rights

If demon spirits are present, it is important that we determine if they have consent to be there. Demons cannot enter a person by choice. There must be some *permission* granted. What are some common reasons demons are allowed to enter?

By far the most common entryway is the consent given for evil spirits to be passed to a child because of the sins of the parents and those of earlier generations. These are referred to as generational or "ancestral curses." Here legal permission for evil spirits to pass from one generation to another is given. We will be talking more about generational curses in a later chapter.

Demons cannot enter without the legal right to do so!

The *good news* is that through *repentance*, such curses can be broken. But again, evil spirits do not leave until they are made to leave. Repentance cancels their permission to be there, but they will leave only if *commanded* to do so. This is why it is so important that we regularly seek forgiveness for our sins (1 John 1:9), which then denies them legal entrance.

> *Stop!* This truth is so important that much review may be necessary for it to become revelation in your spirit!

For example, when one is "born again", your body can still become sick, and your mind, will and emotions which make up your soul, can still be affected adversely. If you suffered with depression or fear before you were "saved," these and other forms of torment will remain without relief unless the unclean spirits are dealt with by casting them out.

During our lifetime, we may have allowed Satan and evil spirits or demons without our knowing, gain access through an open door of sin. Though we may now be spiritually "born again", these unclean spirits do not have to leave and will not leave unless they are cast out. Therefore, any demons that have gained the legal right to our lives in the past *prior to salvation*, will not leave unless we make them leave through the deliverance process.

Knowing the truth about demons can set you free!

But again, demons must have *open doors* to enter a person's life on legal grounds. Although, drugs, alcohol, sexual sin, and occult involvement are most common, there are certain kinds of books, literature, music, and movies that provide a means for demons to enter as well.

For example, if a person has a problem with anger, alcohol, or drugs, or has a particular illness before being saved, that person will still most likely have these afterward. If you had diabetes before you were "saved," you will have it after. If you had mental or emotional concerns before, you will have them afterward. Nevertheless, we can be set free from every form of oppression—addictions, jealousy, lying, deception, lust, grief, and rejection— just to name a few.

Demons must be confronted and made to leave!

As stated earlier, Jesus was very aware of this truth and often confronted demons wherever He went. This is why when He sent out His disciples (Luke 10:1), He clearly told them not only to heal the sick and raise the dead, but to cast out demons. Because of His great compassion for those who were oppressed by the devil, He went about doing good—dealing with unclean spirits on many occasions.

We mentioned that in the gospels of the New Testament, a woman who was bent over with a spirit of infirmity for many years was released from her bondage. A man who could not speak was set free from a mute spirit; the blind and deaf from deaf and dumb spirits, and those with many spirits of sickness, disease, and infirmities were healed as well.

Confronting Satan's Kingdom

When a believer begins to address areas of bondage, using the authority that he or she has been given to resist and confront Satan and his kingdom, this activity of spiritual warfare is referred to as personal or "self-deliverance" (Proverbs 6:5). Through this process, we can keep ourselves and others free from unclean spirits so that we can live life healthily— physically, mentally, emotionally, and spiritually.

Yes, as stated above, all can have a demon or many demons. It's time that we begin to boldly discern and deal with tormenting spirits that seek to oppress every one of us. We have failed to confront these tormentors due to the lack of the truth for far too long. May God help us to shout the truth from the rooftops (Luke 12:3). We must no longer perish for a lack of this knowledge.

> *Stop!* Don't continue on until you have the revelation of this truth in your spirit.

Chapter Review!

1. Everyone has been affected by demons during our lifetime.
2. Demons gain entrance through doorways of sin.
3. Demonic spirits will not leave unless they are commanded to do so.
4. Satan does not have access to the spirit of the believer, but he can inflict harm on the physical body and soul.
5. Be careful not to give Satan the legal right to bring torment and oppression into your life.
6. Demons must be confronted and cast out to achieve total freedom.

Confession of Faith

Let's declare the following confession *out loud* together!

Heavenly Father, I repent of my sins and I look to you for discernment in identifying all demonic activity in my life. Help me not to give the devil any opportunity or legal right to torment or oppress me any further. I renounce Satan and all his works, and I declare myself totally free in Jesus's name. Amen.

For I know that this will turn out for my deliverance through your prayer and the supply of the Spirit of Jesus Christ.

Philippians 1:19

In the next chapter, we will discuss another important question in regard to deliverance ministry concerning one who is not a Christian. Since everyone is in need of deliverance, how does this relate to those who do not have a personal relationship with Jesus Christ?

Chapter 5

Can An Unsaved Person Be Delivered?

And lead us not into temptation; but deliver us from evil.

Luke 11:4

Using Caution

When considering the deliverance ministry of Jesus in setting captives free, we see that Jesus made *no distinction* when casting out demons between the saved and the unsaved, or those who knew Him and those who did not—nor did His disciples prior to Christ's sacrifice on the cross. Yet many who were oppressed by demons were delivered through their ministry.

Always use caution when an unsaved person is seeking deliverance!

However, wisdom would suggest that we use discernment in ministering deliverance when one is not a Christian—simply because of the fact that only a spirit-filled believer, one who has the Holy Spirit dwelling within his spirit, has the power and authority over Satan and every demon in his kingdom. This is why every effort should be taken to encourage an unsaved person to accept Christ as their Savior and Lord—before any attempt is made to minister deliverance.

It is one thing to be set free and quite another to stay free. No one is able to resist demons without the power of the Holy Spirit. Again, this occurs only when one is "born again" spiritually through faith in Jesus Christ. Having a relationship with the Father through His son is *absolutely necessary* in defeating Satan and his kingdom. When considering "self- deliverance," an unsaved person would have no power over demon spirits and, therefore, should not attempt to do so.

One must be 'born again' to have power over demons!

However, since demons must obey the authority that is in the name of Jesus that has been given to every believer, the answer is "yes". An unsaved person can be set free from demonic bondage. If a Christian uses his authority to cast out demons from the life of an unsaved person, they must obey.

As mentioned previously, there are those who consider it wise to be cautious for two reasons: First, without God-given authority, there is no power for an unsaved person to keep departed demons from returning (Luke 11:24). Second, some believe and have found that delivering an unsaved person, in some cases, has done more harm than good. Why is this?

Look to the Holy Spirit for discernment!

Returning Demons

It says in (Matthew 12:43–45) when an unclean spirit is cast out, he can seek to return if nothing has replaced the void that has been created within a person, and he continues to have the legal right to return due to sin. When this occurs the Word of God teaches that others more wicked than himself may enter as well—making things even worse. Let's take a closer look at this portion of Scripture:

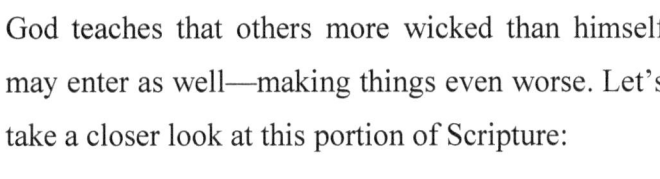

Beware of returning demons!

"When an unclean spirit is gone out of a man, he walketh through dry places, seeking rest, and findeth none. Then he saith, I will return into my house from whence I came out; and when he is come, he findeth it empty, swept, and garnished. Then goeth he, and taketh with himself seven other spirits more wicked than himself, and they enter in and dwell there: and the last state of that man is worse than the first."

This passage suggests that unless a person does what is necessary to stay delivered, administering deliverance to one who is not a Christian is *questionable* indeed. Wisdom would suggest that a person's spirit be delivered first through the "new birth" experience before any attempt is made to deliver their soul and body from demonic captivity. However, this is not always possible. Therefore, we must seek *discernment* from the Holy Spirit in every situation we may encounter.

As we've said before, deliverance ministry should not be taken lightly. Keeping this in mind, perhaps the question should not be

"Can an unsaved person be delivered," but rather "Should that person be delivered without first giving their heart and life to Christ" (John 3:16, 17).

Stop! It is important that we meditate on these things!

A Sober Warning

Notice the following accounts found in (Acts 19:13–17). We are told that a group of Jews were traveling from town to town casting out evil spirits. Having observed the apostle Paul and others doing the same, they tried to use the name of the Lord Jesus saying, "I command you in the name of Jesus whom Paul preaches, to come out!"

We also read of the seven sons of Sceva, and a leading priest as well.

"Then certain Jewish exorcists took it upon themselves to call over them which had evil spirits the name of the Lord Jesus, saying, 'We adjure you by Jesus whom Paul preacheth.' And the evil spirit answered and said, 'Jesus I know, and Paul I know; but who are you'? And the man in whom the evil spirit was, leaped on them, and overcame them, and prevailed against them so that they fled out of that house naked and wounded."

Faith in Jesus Christ is an important prerequisite when entering into deliverance!

Here we see more vividly the importance of knowing the Lord Jesus Christ before attempting to undertake setting yourself or someone else free who is in need of deliverance. Nevertheless, there is no reason to fear any demon when you have the power and authority that is given to every believer in Jesus's name (Luke 10:19).

A Clear Admonition

I cannot overemphasize the importance of this truth. May I once again remind you of the purpose of this writing—to provide you with the knowledge that you need, and clear guidance in the use of that knowledge—as you may seek personal deliverance for yourself and others? The warning remains that we not be *presumptuous* or prone to rush into bold encounters carelessly.

All attempts at deliverance should be taken very seriously!

Again, this writer strongly believes that revelation from the Word of God must be accompanied by a deep commitment to the Lordship of Jesus Christ—having absolute *dependence* upon the Holy Spirit in every situation. We cannot overemphasize this truth. It bears repeating that we should not seek to minister deliverance if at all possible unless a person has truly placed their faith in the Son of God, and has a close *abiding relationship* with Him. Spiritual discernment must be applied in each situation as it presents itself.

Stop! Meditate on the above until it becomes
a deep understanding in your spirit!

Chapter Review!

1. An unsaved person can experience deliverance but should first make a decision to accept Jesus Christ as Savior and Lord.
2. Demons have to leave when commanded by a born-again Christian.
3. Beware of the possibility that demons may try to return.
4. Entering into deliverance ministry should never be taken lightly.

Confession of Faith

Let's make the following confession out loud together!

Lord Jesus, I thank You for Your provision of deliverance. I pray that You will continue to prepare me to be set free, stay free, and teach others to do the same. I will not enter the deliverance process lightly but soberly as I seek the revelation I need from the Holy Spirit. In your name, I pray. Amen.

Those by the way side are they that hear; then cometh the devil, and taketh away the word out of their hearts, lest they should believe and be saved.

Luke 8:12

In the next chapter, we will deal with another important issue concerning the difference between demonic oppression and possession.

Chapter 6

Oppression or Possession?

*Unclean spirits, crying with a loud voice,
came out of many that were possessed with them.*

Acts 8:7

What's the Difference?

Now that we have dealt with the reality of satan's real presence and his desire to bring harm into our lives, let's discuss the difference between the words "oppression and possession". Some have made a distinction between these two terms. There seems to be some controversy as to whether Christians can be possessed, oppressed or both by demons.

No distinction is made in the Greek between oppression and possession!

The word "demonized" is also used when one is in some way under the influence or the power of demons. Some describe such a person as being possessed or oppressed. This verb in the Greek is usually translated in the New Testament—to be possessed or vexed by evil spirits. The fact is that no distinction is made in the original Greek text where this word is used.

Keeping this in mind, some therefore argue that it is useless to make such a distinction—when the Greek word simply means to be *demonized*. Nevertheless, others still suggest that there is a vast difference between being possessed or owned by demons, and being oppressed and tormented.

Regardless, which position one may take, when deliverance is clearly needed, achieving freedom from all demonic activity still remains our goal. However, my purpose in this writing is simply to clarify the terminology to avoid confusion, and allow you to make your own determination.

Two Positions

Among those who do make this distinction, *possession* indicates total control over a person's physical body and mind which are affected by the personality, voice, and actions of a demon or demons that inhabit that body. Demons or unclean spirits can influence human beings in many ways.

In demonic *oppression*, one's behavior, personality, attitudes, and desires can also be affected. However, a person retains control over his physical body and mind. Most are unaware that when oppressed, behavior is often influenced by demonic spirits. Though Satan realizes he cannot take total control of a person's life through oppression, he will seek to gain territory wherever possible.

For the purpose of this writing, when speaking of all demonic activity, we will use the word "oppression"—keeping in mind that all have been demonized in the past, present, and will be in the future.

Stop! Let's meditate once again on the above before going on!

Is My Problem Demonic?

It is important that we receive discernment as to the presence and nature of evil spirits in our lives. We can detect evil spirits by observing behaviors and symptoms that may be manifesting. Carefully consider the following seven possible *indications* that deliverance is needed:

Beware of indications that deliverance is needed!

1. Destructive emotions and attitudes:
   (envy, jealousy, rage, hatred, anger, revenge, fear, self-pity, grief, unforgiveness, pride, impatience, bitterness, depression, withdrawal, worry, inferiority, rejection, self-rejection, isolation, insecurity, inadequacy, etc.)
2. Disturbances in the mind:
   (sudden changes in mood or lifestyle, mental torment, procrastination, indecision, compromise, confusion, doubt, unbelief, loss of memory, etc.)
3. Inappropriate speech:
   (lying, cursing, criticism, mockery, gossip, etc.)
4. Unclean thoughts and actions:
   (sex outside of marriage, lust, fornication, adultery, homosexuality, bestiality, pornography, etc.)
5. Bondages and addictions:
   (drugs, alcohol, overeating, smoking, etc.)
6. Physical sicknesses and infimities:
   (insomnia, migraines, tumors, paralysis, deafness, blindness, various diseases, etc.)
7. Involvement with religious error:

When you struggle or feel compelled to do something you don't want to do, you are being demonized!

(cults, false religions, false teachings, etc.)

(See Section: "Demonic Groupings")

Stop! Do take time to meditate on the above!

Finding the Source

Demonic spirits may cause certain behaviors and destructive emotions!

Demonic oppression can begin when we are children and continue throughout our adult lives. Our environment, the things we have been exposed to and our ancestry do have an effect. Demons start working on our soul with our emotions, ungodly attitudes, and actions at an early age. Therefore, if you cannot seem to get the victory in an area, and you keep finding yourself struggling with the same issue or issues over and over again, this would suggest the presence of a *demonic stronghold*.

For example, if you are experiencing difficulty controlling certain emotions such as a desire to destroy yourself or someone else—most likely there are spirits of suicide, murder, and death affecting the emotions in your soul. Or if you are struggling with lustful thoughts and have a strong desire to engage in sexual activity outside of marriage, a number of unclean spirits are most likely at the root of your problem. Jesus wants you to be free from such tormenting spirits, and you can be free if you want to be.

Partial Deliverance

Before closing this chapter, let me take a moment to share what happened when a Christian woman who had been wonderfully used of God in the past as a missionary, came to us for help due to strong oppression that had

Never settle for less than total deliverance!

begun to take away her sense of well-being and *quality of life*. She shared that she was finding it difficult to function due to severe depression and fear. When questioned further, it was discovered that she had attended a new church and even had become a member. Gradually, she began to see and hear some things that did not agree with her Christian beliefs. It was then that debilitating emotional problems began to manifest over a period of months.

She came several times for deliverance prayer ministry. During that time, a number of demonic spirits were successfully cast out, and she was greatly relieved. However, it was clear that further ministry was needed in order for her to be completely set free from all oppression. Unfortunately, she chose not to return. When I saw her some time later, she was still suffering from much torment and it seemed to a greater degree. I believe this occurred because she had experienced only a partial deliverance. It is my prayer that you will never settle for anything less than *total deliverance* as a way of life.

Demonic oppression is a very serious matter. It is something we have all lived with during the course of our lives. However, the *good news* is that we do not have to allow this to continue one day longer. The choice is ours. For God has said, "I have set before you life and death, blessing and cursing; therefore choose life, that both you and your descendants may live" (Deuteronomy 30:19).

Stop! Please take time here to meditate once again!

Chapter Review!

1. Possession indicates total control or ownership of a person's being by the personality, voice, and actions of an unclean spirit or spirits.
2. Oppression occurs when one's emotions, attitudes, and behavior are strongly influenced by demon spirits.
3. There is a need for deliverance when you continue to struggle with something that you just can't get the victory over that is causing you torment.
4. It's important that every area of bondage be identified and every demon be cast out in order to achieve a complete and ongoing deliverance.
5. Choose life and freedom from all demonic activity and never settle for anything less.

Confession of Faith

Let's make the following confession *out loud* together!

Deliverance is an ongoing process that must be maintained with diligence!

> Lord Jesus, I come to You today seeking to understand the source of my problems. I pray for discernment so that I can identify every demonic spirit that may be tormenting me physically, mentally, emotionally or spiritually. I want to be totally set free from all oppression so that I can live the life you have given me to enjoy.

Therefore, I choose to give no place to the devil, and I declare I will diligently resist any attempt to hold me captive. Help me to stay free so that I can help others to do the same. In Your name, I pray. Amen.

To loose the bands of wickedness, to undo the heavy burdens, and let the oppressed go free.

Isaiah 58:6

In the next chapter, we will discuss how you have been given all power and authority over all the power of the enemy so that you can live life free of all torment.

Chapter 7

The Authority of Every Believer

Behold I give you power to tread on serpents and scorpions, and over all the power of the enemy and nothing shall by any means harm you.

Luke 10:19

God-given Authority

In the early days of the church, it was assumed that every believer was capable of obtaining freedom through deliverance. Jesus clearly *commissioned all* saying, "In my name they will drive out demons" (Mark 16:17). There is no evidence that a Christian had to be ordained to cast out evil spirits or have any *special training*. Unfortunately, as time went on deliverance ministry became more and more *restricted*.

Every believer has all power and authority over the enemy!

Therefore, when entering into any discussion on deliverance, there is *good news* in knowing that God has given every "born again" Christian the *authority* and *power* that is needed over all the power of the enemy. We read in (Matthew 10:7, 8) that Jesus commanded His twelve disciples and later seventy-two others to go and preach saying,

"The kingdom of heaven is at hand. Heal the sick, cleanse the lepers, raise the dead, cast out demons; freely ye have received, freely give."

Today, it is our *relationship* with Jesus Christ that enables us to *exercise* this same authority as a result of His relationship with His Heavenly Father. Jesus said, "All power and authority is given unto me in heaven and in earth" (Matthew 28:18).

A Reawakening

At the beginning of the twentieth century, there was an awakening among Pentecostals about supernatural gifts—including the power to cast out evil spirits. The rediscovery of the need for many people to be set free from demonic oppression, manifested under the ministry of a

Mass deliverance will set many free from demonic oppression!

number of church leaders like Derek Prince and Don Basham, who practiced *mass deliverance* with whole congregations. Despite much opposition, they felt they had to do something regardless of criticism—to help the many victims of demonic oppression at that time.

Tragically, this same crisis situation exists today as well. Spiritual warfare and deliverance is simply not taught in most churches and among God's people in general. Nevertheless, more are being raised up by the Holy Spirit because of the cry of Father's heart for His people who are perishing needlessly. It is urgent that the *truth be revisited* and every believer be made aware of "personal deliverance." We must first obtain our own freedom from demons in our personal lives, and then reach out and help others to do the same.

Righteous Indignation

"Authority" may be defined as the power to act on behalf of another. Every Christian has been given authority to aggressively plunder Satan's kingdom. Jesus has given us His power to carry on His ministry and build His kingdom. To be given this spiritual authority, it requires that we humble ourselves under God's authority. As we do, we are to resist *spiritual principalities* and *powers* that control the lives of people and the world system in which we live.

With a violent spirit stand against every assault of the enemy!

(Matthew 11:12) says that "the kingdom of heaven suffereth violence, and the violent take it by force." This means that with *righteous indignation* and a *violent spirit*, we are to stand against every assault of the enemy—taking back everything that's been stolen and destroyed by the devil and his demons.

Again, we must remember that our battle is not with people, but with demonic spirits that operate through people (Ephesians 6:12). Knowing this, we can have great compassion because we understand that it is the enemy who is behind everything that is evil in our world.

Fearless Confrontation

John Paul Jackson in his book *Needless Casualties of War* states, "We are called to exercise our God-given authority and power to destroy the works of Satan." The authority of the believer is a settled fact clearly commanded in the Scriptures, and it is important that every believer act upon this powerful truth—for oneself and for the welfare of others.

I am aware of the reluctance of many to get involved in any confrontation with demons, and that the main reason is most likely the fear of the unknown. Mark Bubeck states in his book, *The Adversary*, "The enemy will be relentless in using every opportunity to gain a foothold in any way possible with various afflictions and subtle bondages." Nevertheless, we must strongly resist any attempt of the enemy to bring harm into our lives.

Stop! Let's take a moment and meditate on the authority of every believer!

Binding and Loosing

Binding and loosing is always done in the spirit realm. We have been given the power to bind and loose according to the will of God. (Psalm 149:8, 9) says we are to bind the enemy with the judgments that are written in the Word

When we don't use our authority, Satan is free to do great harm!

of God. Standing on (Matthew 18:18), we can declare that what has already been bound in heaven, we can bind on earth, and what has been loosed in heaven, we can loose on earth.

Scripture declares that Jesus has given us power to bind and loose in reference to Satan. Binding and loosing is an effective means of hindering the enemy's plans to steal, kill, and destroy all that is yours (John 10:10). When one is tied up or bound with a rope, with persistence that person will most likely eventually work free. In the same way, when Satan is bound, although it is temporary, you can bind him again and again and all who are a part of his kingdom.

(1 John 3:8) says that Jesus came to the earth to destroy the works of the devil, and we are to do the same works that Jesus did and more (John 14:12). The *principle of binding* and *loosing* works today just as it always has. We must use this weapon with confidence because it works.

When we receive Jesus Christ into our lives, we receive His abiding presence and glorious power which includes power over evil spirits (Matthew 28:18). Every believer has been given the power and authority to ward off every attack of the enemy. Unfortunately, the average Christian is not fully aware that they have everything they need to bind up Satan and his followers. Therefore, tragically many believers remain in bondage.

Binding and loosing is a powerful tool to use in resisting the devil!

(Matthew 16:19) says that Jesus has given us keys to the kingdom of heaven, and whatever you bind on earth will be bound in heaven, and whatever you loose on earth will be loosed in heaven. Every believer has the authority to bind and loose the demonic kingdom in this world.

The word "binding" means to confine, restrain, or restrict; while "loosing" means to release or set free from restraint. These are two important tools that we must use against the enemy when attacked. Be assured that Satan can do no harm if we walk in the power and authority God has given to us as believers. God expects us to take the *offensive* and drive out all spiritual wickedness wherever it is found—in our homes, schools, churches, communities—everywhere that the kingdom of darkness is operating. We have an important part to play in this battle between the kingdoms of light and darkness.

We are not to give the devil place through a *lack of resistance*. He can have no power over us unless we give it to him. (James 4:7) says, "Draw near to God, resist the devil and he will flee from you." When we don't do anything about rebuking the devil and *standing our ground*, nothing will be accomplished, and he will continue to do everything he can to destroy us and those we love.

Strongly stand your ground and demand your release!

You must actively bind the powers of darkness, command them to leave, and make it clear that you have *full authority* over them—based on the Word of God (Luke 10:19). In areas of bondage, strongly demand your release from everything that has held you captive—always making it clear that when you command, demons must obey.

> *Stop!* Continue to meditate on your authority in Christ until this truth becomes a revelation in your spirit!

Power in the Name of Jesus

The fact is that every evil spirit is subject to the name of Jesus according to Scripture. Why is this? (Ephesians 1:17–22) expresses the depth of power that God has given His son Jesus—for it says that He has "put all things under His feet." Also, (Philippians 2:9–11) tells us "That at the name of Jesus every knee shall bow, of things in heaven, and things in the earth, and things under the earth." Therefore, we see that all are subject to the power that is in the name of Jesus.

The name of Jesus is another powerful weapon you must use against the enemy!

According to (John 16:23), Jesus Himself gives us the authority to use His name for He said, "Whatsoever you ask the Father in my name, He will give it to you." Again, in (John 14:12) we are told by Jesus that if we have faith in Him, we will do what He has done and even *greater things*." "Ask and you shall receive, seek and you shall find. Knock and it shall be opened unto you" (John 16:24). Yes, every believer in Christ has authority to use Jesus's name, and there is no evil force we cannot overcome.

It is important that we grasp this truth as we continue to prepare ourselves to engage in personal deliverance. We must pray, decree, declare, and use our authority—knowing that *power is released* when we declare the name of Jesus.

> *Stop!* Let's take time here to prayerfully meditate on this truth.

Vision of the Second Heaven

Frank Hammond in his book, *Saints of War*, wrote of the powerful vision of Jay Lee who was taken by Jesus into the second heaven which he was told was Satan's headquarters.

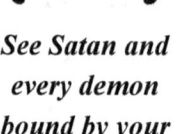

See Satan and every demon bound by your words!

"Entering a long dark chamber, Jay Lee saw a long table. Satan was present at one end of the table as a flame of fire—along with other demonic spirits positioned at each side of the room.

With great boldness Jay declared, 'I bind you all in the name of Jesus.' Suddenly, Jay saw gold chains shoot out of his fingertips and wrap around each demon spirit in the room. Satan became furious and said, 'Don't ever do that again.' Jay realized that when a believer binds the enemy, this act binds Satan and his kingdom." This is a *powerful revelation*!

"Then the Lord took Jay into a large field where below many demons were bound. Jesus explained that these were once very active, but members of the body of Christ had bound them up. Jay also saw spirits binding up people who could hardly move. However, other people who knew who they were in Christ, when they used their authority, their bindings fell off.

Returning to the chamber they found other demons frantically trying to free Satan from his chains—but to no avail. Then Jay noticed that some of the chains on Satan were rusting off. The Lord explained that believers who had put them there had lost their faith. When this happens in time, those chains will rust and Satan will be free once again."

I have included this account so that we may better understand the power that has been given to us in the spirit realm. We must recognize who we are and whose we are, and actively use our authority to bind up the enemy. May God give us the resolve to actively confront Satan and his kingdom as we envision what's taking place in the *realm of the spirit.*

Stop! I encourage you not to go on to the next section without spending time meditating on the above vision. This truth needs to be etched in your spirit by the Holy Spirit!

Examples of Things to Bind and Loose

Actively use your authority to bind the enemy!

The following list will assist you as you use your authority to bind and loose. When taking action against the enemy, you need to bind Satan's actions and *loose God's provision* in its place. Take time to declare the following on a regular basis over your life and those you love. The *words we speak* have great power to save, heal, and deliver all who are sorely oppressed by the devil.

Bind	Loose
Death	Abundant Life
Stealing	Restitution
Destruction	Restoration
Deception	Truth
Hatred	Love
Rejection	Acceptance
Weakness	Strength
Depression	Joy
Illness	Divine Health
Unforgiveness	Forgiveness
Cursing	Blessing
Poverty	Prosperity
Torment	Peace
Fear	Power, Love, A Sound Mind

Taking Action

Consider the following two steps and remember to always bind and loose in Jesus's name! When you are confronted with an unclean spirit, speak *out loud* what you are binding—recognizing it as a demon and not a person.

Step 1. Speak to what you are binding.

"_____, I bind you in the name of Jesus."

Step 2. Loose in the same manner.

"_____, I loose you in the name of Jesus."

Stop! Take a moment to practice binding and loosing!

Chapter Review!

1. God expects every believer to use the authority He has provided to destroy the works of the devil.
2. If you know Jesus Christ as a believer, you have all the authority that is needed to bind evil and loose righteousness.
3. With righteous indignation demand everything that has been stolen and destroyed be restored.
4. Strongly resist any attempt of the enemy to bring harm into your life.
5. Binding and loosing is an effective means of resisting the enemy.
6. Do not give place to the devil through a lack of resistance.
7. The name of Jesus has great power to deliver you.

Confession of Faith

Let's make the following confession *out loud* together!

Heavenly Father, in the name of Your son, Jesus, I thank You for the authority and power You have given me over all the power of the enemy. I now resist Satan and his evil works in my life, and I declare that nothing shall by any means harm me. I come in the full authority of the kingdom of God and the name of Jesus, and I declare that I am free from the oppressive hand of the enemy. I will actively bind and loose and give no place to demonic spirits in Jesus's name, I pray. Amen

He that is begotten by God keepeth himself, And that wicked one toucheth him not.

1 John 5:18b

In the next chapter, we will consider some of the most common *strongholds* that can greatly hinder your deliverance.

Chapter 8

Dealing with Strongholds

How can one enter into a strong man's house, and spoil his goods, except he first bind the strong man? and then he will spoil his house.

Matthew 12:29

What is a Stronghold?

Jesus clearly called any demonic presence a stronghold or strongman. Strongholds can be overcome by any Christian who is willing to put forth the effort that is needed to confront and utterly destroy the enemy. Again, we must use the strategies and tools that the Lord has provided. These *weapons of warfare* are effective in pulling down every stronghold.

"The weapons of our warfare are not carnal, but mighty through God to the pulling down of strongholds; casting down imaginations, and every high thing (proud thing) that exalteth or raises itself against the knowledge of God, and bringing into captivity every thought (capturing every thought and making it give up and obey Christ) to the obedience of Christ" (2 Corinthians 10:4,5).

The word "stronghold" gives the idea of something held safely inside fortifications. Therefore, anything of a troubling nature which Satan holds securely and is surrounded with strong defenses, is a stronghold that must be attacked and destroyed. In destroying every stronghold, we must penetrate all of its *defenses*. Each barrier or defense requires a unique method of attack. Therefore, in order to gain an understanding of any stronghold, we need to determine how the defenses came into being. Again, it is through sin or disobedience to God that a stronghold is established.

So what are these individual defenses in a stronghold? According to the above scripture, they are *imaginations*, high things, and thoughts. These are products of the mind or thought processes. The New Living Translation makes this passage more understandable. We are to knock down the strongholds of human reasoning, destroy false arguments and every proud obstacle that keeps people from knowing the truth—taking captive every *rebellious thought* in obedience to Christ.

Every stronghold must be destroyed to achieve ongoing deliverance!

> *Stop!* Make sure you understand
> the concept of a stronghold.

Closing Open Doors

I trust that you are now aware that Satan and his kingdom are very real and have always posed a threat to your well-being and those you love. As we prepare for the deliverance process, it is important to understand that during the course of our lifetime, open doors have allowed demonic activity to oppress us in a number of ways—through physical, mental, and emotional torment, sickness, and troubling circumstances.

Let's look at a very important truth. The apostle Paul clearly stated that we are the *determining factor* whether the devil can operate in our lives or not. "Neither give place to the devil" (Ephesians 4:27). This means that we are to leave no room or *opportunity* for the devil to gain a foothold. The fact is that when we allow openings in our spiritual lives, the devil feels he has the right to take advantage of us.

However, if we keep the doors closed, he cannot do what he would like to do.

We first see this "open door principle" in (Genesis 4:7), when the Lord told Cain, "If thou dost not well, sin lieth at the door. And unto thee shall be his desire, and thou shall rule over him." Like you and I, Cain had a choice. Because he

Open doors are an invitation for the enemy to oppress you!

chose to open the door to jealousy, Satan led him to murder his brother Abel.

Know that sin is progressive. One thing leads to another until we find ourselves in deep trouble. For this reason, we must learn to close those doors before they develop into a *stronghold* that can bring destruction into our lives.

An open door can occur in several ways—when others sin against us through such things as abandonment, abuse, rejection, and all kinds of ill treatment; through ancestral sin from previous generations which is passed down through the *bloodline*—such as inherited curses and addictions; and finally as a result of various sinful practices that we have done ourselves such as sexual sin, dishonesty, and willful acts of disobedience. These open doors have allowed the enemy to move in and out of our lives, due to a lack of knowledge and understanding on our part (Hosea 4:6). This *lack of knowledge* has caused great harm to come to us and our loved ones.

Beware of any open doors that must be closed through repentance!

During the deliverance process, we must individually seek to find these open doors and close them once and for all so that we can experience the freedom in Christ that was purchased for us on Calvary's cross. Through deliverance ministry, God wants to set you free and teach you how to *stay free* on a daily basis. Again, this is the goal of our ministry.

Satan and his demons have been chasing and tormenting you and me for a very long time. However, through the process of personal deliverance, we can take back all that has been stolen. Then with this knowledge, we can help to set others free as well (Mark 16:18).

> *Stop!* Take time to consider any open doors
> that you may be aware of in your life!

Possessing Your Strongholds

In this process of closing open doors, you must first determine the specific strongholds that have affected your life—bringing you into captivity. A stronghold might also be defined as a "wall of resistance" to the truth or any form of bondage. If you are struggling with an addiction, rebellion, fear, or insecurity for example, these are a few very real strongholds that will need to be addressed.

Confront every stronghold with perseverance until you are totally free!

Using the *list of strongholds* found in the back of the book, carefully and prayerfully circle those that you struggle with on a continuing basis. This is not an exhaustive list by any means. However, during the deliverance process, you will need to confront every stronghold, and any others that the Holy Spirit may reveal to you.

Again, do take time to consider the possibility of any *open doors* as well. Each of these can very definitely hinder you in obtaining the freedom that you desire. Take time to *make a list*.

The following are found to be among the most common:

> *(unforgiveness, bitterness, resentment, hatred, unconfessed sin, pride, involvement with the occult, sexual sin, and idolatry—anyone or thing that you are putting before the Lord such as your family, money, home, job, and children.)*

> > *Stop!* It is important that you spend time identifying any strongholds and open doors!

Healed of Schizophrenia

Before we close this chapter, let's listen to Nick Griesmann's amazing story of deliverance from mental illness and the hope that there is in Christ for all who suffer with various forms of physical, mental and emotional torment.

Desperately seeking help from various local churches, it seemed that no one had the answers that could set him free. Turning to God and the Scriptures, he learned that he could actually bring down strongholds in the mind that were causing confusion and the voices that tormented him constantly.

He states that through prayer and confessing his sins, he learned from the Word of God that those who believe and are saved have the power to cast out demons in the name of Jesus. Laying his hands on his own body, he literally was set free as he used his authority to cast out various evil spirits. Nick boldly proclaims that you can do the same.

Chapter Review!

1. Anything that is troubling and causes you emotional or physical torment is a stronghold.
2. The enemy can gain entrance through open doors caused by sin.
3. It is important that you determine the strongholds that have been affecting your life and any open doors that need to be closed.
4. Many unacceptable behaviors have as their source a demonic spirit or spirits that when cast out, will give you the relief and freedom that you need.

Confession of Faith

Let's make the following confession *out loud* together!

> Heavenly Father, help me to discern any strongholds or open doors that need to be closed. I repent of every sin, and I desire to live in a way that is pleasing to You. I sincerely want to be set free from everything that has held me in bondage. I now renounce every unclean spirit that has entered my life. Thank you for providing deliverance for me through Calvary's cross. In Jesus's name, I pray. Amen.

> *The righteous cry out, and the Lord hears,*
> *And delivers them out of all their troubles.*
>
> Psalm 34:17

In the next chapter, we will discuss *generational curses* which can and often are the source of many of our problems.

Chapter 9

Generational Curses

*He whom thou blessest is blessed,
and he whom thou cursest is cursed.*

Numbers 22:6

Ancestral Sins

The topic of deliverance would not be complete without addressing the subject of curses, which can bring great harm to an individual and their loved ones. A "curse" is defined as an evil or misfortune in a person's life due to sin. A curse causes sorrow of heart

When we choose to sin, family and future generations are affected!

and gives demonic spirits the *legal right* to enter the bloodline of a family and carry out their wicked plans.

We need to examine closely any inherited weaknesses from our family lineage. Our ancestors may have done things we are completely unaware of that can still affect us today. (Exodus 20:5) states that the Lord visits the iniquity of the fathers upon the children unto the *third* and *fourth generations*.

When we look to God for help, we must understand that we play a very important role in determining our present and our future.

According to (Romans 13:12–14), we are not to fulfill the desires of our flesh which takes willpower. Sins of the flesh such as fornication, adultery, and divorce do affect not only ourselves but our loved ones as well.

Stop! Let's think on these things!

Kinds of Curses

It is believed that there are three categories of curses—generational curses, self-imposed curses, and curses put upon others by those who are involved with the occult.

Curses remain in effect until they are broken through the deliverance process!

"Generational curses" are passed down to individuals because of the sins of their ancestors—again, visiting the sins of the fathers upon future generations (Exodus 34:7).

"Self-imposed curses" enter our lives through sins we have committed ourselves. Curses can bring bondage, sickness, pain, sorrow, and shame which take away our quality of life, and sometimes even result in physical death. Therefore, it is imperative that every curse be *confronted*, renounced and destroyed in order to gain full deliverance.

Biblical Examples

It's important to understand that just as there are physical laws that govern this world, there are *spiritual laws* that have been established as well. We see in Scripture, examples of curses that were passed down to future generations.

Lamech, a descendant of Cain who murdered his brother Abel (Genesis 4:10,11), also killed a man (Genesis 4:23,24).

Abraham lied when he said Sarah was not his wife for fear of his life (Genesis 12:13), and Isaac his son lied about his wife Rebekah for the same reason (Genesis 26:7).

Jacob lied to his father Isaac that he was his brother Esau (Genesis 27:19).

King David committed sexual sin with Bathsheba (2 Samuel 11:2–5), as did Rahab the harlot who was among David's ancestors (Matthew 1:5) (Joshua 6:25).

Stop! Take a moment and consider any generational curses you may be aware of in your family!

Redeemed From the Curse

Despite this truth, there is *good news!* The Scriptures declare that we can be redeemed from every curse because Christ has redeemed us from the curse of the law— being made a curse for us (Galatians 3:13). When Jesus Christ shed His blood for the forgiveness of our sins on the cross, as a believer in Christ, every curse in our lives can be broken as we confess our sins and the sins of our ancestors (1 John 1:9).

Curses need to be *identified*—just like any stronghold that may be present in our lives. As we use the authority that we have been given, every curse can be destroyed, and we can be set free from all torment and oppression of the enemy.

Right living brings a blessing while sin brings a curse!

The Sin Connection

When one is *born again*, our eternal destiny is put under the blood of Jesus. However, if there is sin connected to our lives individually or generationally, unless renounced the enemy has a legal right to cause torment in different ways. However, as we deal with all sin, we can find freedom from satan's attempts to bring harm to ourselves and others.

Again, the following possible sins can bring a curse: (unforgiveness, judging others, stealing, occult involvement, sexual sin, drugs, alcoholism, broken vows, pornography, divorce, and rebellion—just to name a few).

> *Stop!* As you meditate, consider the above as they may apply, and make a list of any curses you may be aware of.

Word Curses

Curses can also be spoken. It is important to understand that the words we speak have great power to transform our lives for good or evil. There is both life and death in the tongue (Proverbs 18:21). Demonic word curses can be cast upon Christians when there are doors left open. Wrong words spoken to you, about you, and by you, remain in effect unless challenged.

*** Beware of negative words and actions which are the source of much evil!***

These can be spoken throughout your lifetime by those around you—your mate, parents, siblings, friends, and coworkers.

The issue is not necessarily by whom they are spoken, but rather the serious harm that they can produce in our lives when not acknowledged and resisted. If your soul comes into *agreement* or accepts negative words when spoken, great pain can result which can hinder both your emotional and physical well-being.

Once again, the *good news* is that words can loose their effects upon our lives when we use the authority that has been given to us as believers in Christ. Remember, to *loose* means to smash or destroy. It doesn't matter whether you know or don't know the specific negative words that have been spoken over your life. The principle of binding and loosing will still work in nullifying their effects. (Review: Chapter 7 "The Authority of Every Believer")

Stop! Meditate on the harm that can result from our words!

Curses from Others

Many Christians have deceived themselves into believing that a curse cannot affect them because they are *born again*.

It's important to determine the cause or source of a curse!

However, a believer can have an open door due to sin and not be aware of it. When this is the case, Satan can cause havoc in our lives by using others to bring torment and oppression by the words they speak. Again, some examples are chronic sickness and disease, physical and emotional pain, financial problems, accidents, defeat and discouragement, and other areas of loss.

Nevertheless, keep in mind that God is our source, strength, and protector. We must focus on His power and love, and never fear the enemy. Through Jesus we have all power and authority over Satan and his kingdom. We can be free and stay free from every curse, as we stay focused on Him, His love and His faithfulness.

Am I Under a Curse?

Here are a few additional thoughts that you may relate to in determining if what you have been experiencing is the result of a curse or merely unfortunate circumstances that have affected your life adversely. A "curse" may also be defined as inflicting harm or injury upon oneself or another person by supernatural means. Another way of describing the presence of a curse is that there seems somehow to be a dark shadow over your life which came out of your past—but you may not know how, where or when it occurred.

It may seem that you are being hindered in some way as you go through life, and things just never seem to work out for you. Every time you are about to succeed—something intervenes and steals your blessing. You may have all the qualifications for success, but somehow time after time it always seems to escape you. If any of these describe you, deliverance is the key to your *breakthrough*.

Never fear the enemy or give him place to do you harm!

The following have been suggested as indications that there is a curse over a person's life. These can also be found in chapter 28 of the book of Deuteronomy in the Old Testament of the Bible.

1. Mental and emotional breakdowns, suicide and insanity.
2. Repeated or chronic sicknesses especially when hereditary.
3. Female problems such as miscarriages or inability to conceive.
4. A history of marriage and family breakdowns.
5. Generational poverty. Repeated accidents within a family or individual.
6. History of suicides or unnatural deaths in a family.
7. Debilitating forms of fear (heights, closed spaces, people, failure etc.).
8. Barrenness or anything destroyed or lost.

There is always a cause behind every curse that needs to be discovered!

(See lists of "Demonic Groups" at the back of the book)

Stop! Let's earnestly meditate on the above!

Reasons for Curses

A curse cannot take effect without a reason. Wherever there is a curse at work, a "cause" can be found. Discovering the cause can bring release. The causes for the most common curses that can afflict our lives are listed below. It's important that you know the source of any curse that may be present in your life. *Serious consequences* can affect your children, children's children, and even your great-grandchildren. These also apply to strongholds as well—some of which we have already discussed.

1. Involvement with the occult through witchcraft, divination, and sorcery.
2. Injustice toward the helpless through abortion.
3. Wrong sexual practices.
4. Evil perpetrated against Israel and the Jewish people.
5. Trusting in man's ability rather than God.
6. Robbing God with the tithe.
7. Word curses spoken by ourselves or others through vows taken or broken.
8. Entering into ungodly covenants or relationships.
9. Aligning with false religions and religious practices.
10. Ungodly wisdom, words, and prayers that seek to manipulate, pressure, and control behavior.

From Curse to Blessing

Before closing this chapter, it is important that you follow the steps as outlined below in order to experience a release from any curse that may be present in your life or the lives of others. Remember, our goal is to walk in the blessings of the Lord and not under demonic oppression.

It is important that you practice these steps as a way of life!

1. *Confess* your faith in Christ and in His sacrifice on your behalf.
2. *Recognize* your problem and its cause.
3. *Repent* (turn away from) all rebellion and sin.
4. *Confess* your sins and the sins of your ancestors.
5. *Forgive* all who have sinned against you and claim your forgiveness.
6. *Renounce* all contact with the occult or with secret societies—with each curse and any ungodly relationships that may have opened the door for a curse to be visited upon you.
7. *Break the power* of every generational curse one at a time in the name of Jesus.
8. *Resist* every attempt of Satan to keep you under any curse.

(See Section: "Deliverance Prayers")

Delivered from the Curse of Witchcraft

The curse of witchcraft which is a *controlling spirit* is very prevalent in many families today, and is passed down from previous generations. This curse when visited upon an individual is debilitating and causes much emotional pain, which in turn can affect the physical body with sickness and disease. It is accompanied by spirits of *manipulation* and *possessiveness* with the intent to bind up and take captive in order to fulfill one's own desires—at the expense of another.

When this curse is discovered like any other, it can be destroyed. We have found that it often occurs between a mother and her daughter, a father and his son and among siblings. However, when one is driven by a controlling spirit, it can be visited within any kind of relationship—even between friends and co-workers.

Thankfully, we have seen devastated individuals set free as they are taught to take back their lives through deliverance ministry.

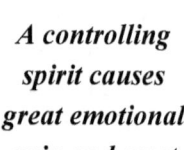

Where there is a curse in operation, there is help available. Don't let another day go by in torment. Too many continue to *suffer needlessly* for a lack of the knowledge that can set them free. This is our heart's desire and our passion—to bring healing and deliverance to all who suffer in our midst.

A controlling spirit causes great emotional pain and must be cast out!

In order to meet this tremendous need, healing deliverance prayer centers must be raised up which is the mandate of this ministry. We covet your prayers!

Chapter Review!

1. Jesus has redeemed you from every curse becoming a curse for you.
2. Bind and loose the effect of every curse with the authority given you in Jesus's name.
3. Repent and turn away from all sin and close the door to all demonic activity.
4. Wrong words spoken to you, about you, and by you can result in a curse and must be resisted and destroyed in the name of Jesus.
5. If you are in torment, don't let another day go by without seeking the help that you need.

Stop! There is much to consider before going on to the next chapter

Confession of Faith

Let's declare the following confession *out loud* together!

> Lord Jesus, I believe that on the cross You took upon Yourself every curse. I now repent and turn away from all sin, closing every door to Satan and his evil works. I renounce and break the power of every curse over myself and my family, and with the authority You have given me, I break every generational curse that has come down to me through my ancestors. I declare myself free in Your mighty name. Amen

Behold, I set before you today a blessing and a curse: the blessing, if you obey...and the curse, if you do not obey.

Deuteronomy 11:26–28

In the next chapter, we will discuss the danger of ungodly soul ties which when broken will release you from much torment and pain.

Chapter 10

Deliverance from Ungodly Soul Ties

*The highway of the upright is to depart from evil:
he that keepeth his way preserveth his soul.*

Proverbs 16:17

Harmful Relationships

In the realm of the spirit, soul ties are created when we enter into relationships with other people. These soul ties may be good or bad—godly or ungodly. When we enter into *ungodly relationships*, we bring much harm into our lives. When this occurs, an ungodly soul tie is created that must be broken through deliverance ministry.

Soul ties are formed when two or more persons become bonded together emotionally. *Godly soul ties* are based on godly love. Throughout the Word of God, we see healthy soul ties between parents and children, husbands and wives, friends with friends, and Christians with Christians. These godly relationships are a blessing from above.

Ungodly soul ties result from sin when spiritual boundaries set up by God are violated. Such soul ties can open the door for unclean spirits to enter. Examples of ungodly soul ties may include the following:

1. Sexual relationships outside marriage or even within a family which allows lust and perversion to enter.
2. Friends who engage in sinful practices open doors for various bondages and addictions to enter—such as drugs, alcohol, nicotine, and unlawful activities.
3. When parents have difficulty in releasing their control over their children as adults.
4. Prolonged mourning in the death of a loved one can result in much suffering unless the soul tie with that person is severed.
5. When sexual sin results in the conceiving of a child outside of marriage or/an abortion takes place.
6. Ungodly soul ties can also travel down the bloodline within a family and transfer at death.
7. Unhealthy relationships within a church family can produce much emotional pain.
8. Involvement with occult practices such as hypnosis can open doors for demons to enter.

Ungodly relationships create ungodly soul ties!

Stop! Let's carefully consider the above ungodly soul ties and any you may be aware of in your own life!

Breaking Ungodly Soul Ties

Breaking harmful soul ties will set you free from much emotional pain. It is important to *make a list* of these ties that need to be broken. You may need to ask God to reveal to you every ungodly soul tie created throughout your lifetime.

These are family members or people from your past or present that have said and done

To achieve freedom every ungodly relationship and soul tie must be broken!

things causing you much harm—perhaps through abusive behaviors, rejection, and abandonment issues. These things will stay with you the rest of your life unless the ungodly soul ties are dealt with and broken.

Only God knows all the influences you need to address. God wants to see you set free in every area of your life. You can trust the Holy Spirit to bring to your mind those who have touched your life in such a way that has devastated your physical, mental, emotional, and even spiritual well-being—opening doors to the demonic.

Seek the Holy Spirit's help in remembering all past ungodly relationships!

Steps to Freedom

The following steps will help you break every ungodly soul tie.

1. *Repent* and *confess* all sin asking God for His forgiveness. Declare the following *out loud*.

    "Father, in the name of Your son, Jesus, I now repent of all my sins and I ask You to forgive me for entering into every ungodly relationship. I take back everything I gave to this person and this person took from me."

2. *Break* and *renounce* all ungodly soul ties with (name each person) *out loud*.

    "I declare with the authority given to me in Jesus Christ that I now break and renounce the ungodly soul tie with _____. I command all demonic spirits that entered my life through this relationship to leave me now, and I take back everything I gave to this person and this person took from me, in Jesus's name."

Stop! Use your list and follow the steps above
in breaking every ungodly soul tie!

Chapter Review!

1. Soul ties are created in the realm of the spirit.
2. When we enter into ungodly relationships, a soul tie is created and must be broken.
3. Ungodly soul ties inflict torment when they are not severed.
4. Through repentance and confession, you can be set completely free.

Confession of Faith

Let's make the following confession *out loud* together!

Lord Jesus, thank you for delivering me from the harmful effects of ungodly soul ties. I ask You to forgive my sin as a result of entering these relationships. I renounce every ungodly soul tie from my past and present relationships. Fill my life with the people You approve of and the kind of relationships you want me to have from now on. In Your name, I pray. Amen.

He that getteth wisdom loveth his own soul: he that keepeth understanding shall find good.

Proverbs 19:8

In the next chapter, we will discuss important *guidelines* for deliverance that must be addressed. Following these will help to ensure your personal deliverance.

Chapter 11

Guidelines for Deliverance

When the Spirit of truth has come, He will guide you into all truth;

John 16:13

Careful Consideration

As we continue our discussion of the deliverance process, we need to address important guidelines that need to be emphasized more fully. Let's take a moment here to review that which we have discussed previously and more. What should be your mindset that will help to ensure a positive outcome when seeking to be set free from demonic oppression?

Careful and frequent review is necessary in order to receive the revelation you need deep within your spirit!

1. One who seeks deliverance should have a *personal relationship* with Christ as Savior and Lord, and truly want to be delivered from every form of captivity.

Remember, it is not possible to cast a demon out unless you have had a "new birth" experience supernaturally and have the power of God's Holy Spirit living within your spirit. Once again, I encourage you to make this most important decision to receive Jesus Christ if you haven't already done so.

Let's pray: Father, I know I am a sinner, and I ask you to forgive me for all the wrong things I have done. I truly accept Your son Jesus as my Lord and Savior. Come into my heart and life and save me now. Amen.

This is the most important decision you will ever make in life!

2. It's important to determine if your troubles are caused by demonic spirits whose purpose is to harass and harm you and your family. Again, if you have found no relief in some area and truly desire to be set free, this is an indication that there are *strongholds* at work in your life.
3. Identify any *open doors* that you have become aware of that have given the enemy the legal right to torment and oppress you. These may include unconfessed sin, the sin of those who have sinned against you or the sins of your ancestors such as: unforgiveness, sexual immorality (demons can be transferred through sexual relationships), occult activity, ungodly soul ties, pornography, being hypnotized, abortion, broken vows and much more. It is very important that you take the time to write down any that apply at this time.

Recognize any strongholds or open doors that may be present in your life!

Three Important Steps

There are three steps in deliverance from demonic strongholds that we have touched upon before: repent, renounce, and release.

First, *repentance* means to humbly express sincere sorrow for sins and a willingness to turn away from that sin—while turning to the one who can forgive, heal, and set you free.

You must repent, renounce and release yourself from every demonic stronghold!

Second, to *renounce* means to declare that you will no longer align yourself with the enemy—cancelling any and all agreements previously entered into which are in opposition to the things of God. With the authority God has given you in Jesus's name, shut the door on the devil once and for all—refusing to walk in the ungodly ways of the past.

Finally, *release* is the means by which you loose yourself from any legal right of Satan to bind or torment you—with strong *resistance* (James 4:7). You are declaring that repentance has taken place, the enemy has been renounced, and you have been given in Christ through the power of His resurrection—freedom from every yoke of bondage.

Stop! Understanding these steps requires meditation, review, and practice.

An Important Reminder

Once again, it is critically important to remember to keep in mind when going into battle with the enemy, that you have been given all *authority* over all his power (Luke 10:19).

Though demons will use every opportunity to intimidate and oppose you, as you place your confidence in the Lord (Ephesians 3:12), these signs will follow those who believe. "In My name they will cast out demons" (Mark 16:17).

You may recall that Jesus commended the centurion who believed, that if Jesus just spoke the word, his servant would be healed. This centurion understood the power of authority. We too must also understand and believe in this authority with a humble spirit and thankful heart. In the spirit realm, our authority comes *You have been given all authority over all the power of the enemy!*

from God's strength alone and not our own (Ephesians 6:10).

Stop! Take time to meditate on this truth again.

What is Deliverance Prayer?

Righteous anger is appropriate and necessary in stopping the devil from bringing torment into your life!

When we begin to practice deliverance, know that *deliverance prayer* is much different than what we might consider normal prayer. Usually, when we pray to God for someone else, our eyes are closed, heads are bowed, and our words seek to bring blessing to others. However, during deliverance prayer, our eyes are open and our words are *directed at Satan* and his kingdom.

We are literally coming against the demon or demons that have brought torment into our lives. Let's never forget that demons seek to steal, kill, and destroy every human being on the planet (John 10:10). *Righteous anger* is appropriate when coming against all that is evil. Boldness to confront and put the enemy to flight is quite in order. (Matthew 11:12).

Who Needs Deliverance?

As previously discussed, Christians have an equal *need of deliverance*, as much as those who have yet to acknowledge Jesus Christ as their Lord and Savior. Unfortunately, there are many who live in *ignorance* of the works of Satan. They are unaware of the source of many of their problems— living tragically in much bondage due to sickness, various afflictions, and unacceptable circumstances which remain *unopposed*.

Most permit the enemy to afflict, entrap, spiritually wound, and imprison them unnecessarily. Perhaps through fear or a lack of the knowledge of the truth—God-given authority and power over Satan and his kingdom have been largely *abandoned*. Nevertheless, today more are coming to the knowledge of the truth as God raises up new voices who are boldly shouting the truth from the rooftops (Matthew 10:27). *Waves of Glory Miracle Ministries* is committed and mandated to fulfill this calling as we seek to be about our Father's business.

Needless torment is unacceptable and should no longer be tolerated!

This means that unless *revelatory truth* is taught and acted upon, God's precious people and mankind as a whole will continue to suffer and ultimately perish (Hosea 4:6). So the question remains whether or not we are going to allow ourselves to continue to be *afflicted unnecessarily* or not. God forbid!

No longer can we allow ourselves to be ignorant of Satan's devices!

Let's never forget that a lifestyle of sin gives the enemy access into our lives which can result in needless torment— unless there is true repentance, a renouncing of all that is evil and a breaking away from all that has held us in bondage.

According to (Galatians 5:16–21), it is God's will that we allow the Holy Spirit to guide our lives—rather than our fleshly nature. The Holy Spirit wants to give us His desires. The need to be free from demonic influence, oppression, and control is our God-given right.

Stop! There's much here to think about.

When is Deliverance Needed?

Take time to determine your need for deliverance!

Many times we are in need of deliverance, but we fail to recognize the *source* of our problems. We may be unaware of the real reason we find ourselves struggling with harmful circumstances. However, as we review these areas, we can be set free from much affliction—as we seek deliverance for ourselves and others.

Let's consider the following *open doors* through which Satan can enter and cause us great harm. Mark or circle any that may apply to your own life. Again, this list is not intended to be exhaustive. There may be other areas that are not mentioned that you need to address as well.

1. Anyone who has a history with the occult, Satanism, and witchcraft.
2. Anyone coming from a background of ancestral worship of other gods.
3. Anyone who has been involved with the New Age movement.
4. Anyone struggling with sexual identity, immorality, or perversion.
5. Anyone suffering with an addiction or uncontrollable habit of some kind.
6. Anyone experiencing sexual intercourse in dreams.
7. Anyone who has invoked a curse upon oneself with words spoken in anger or ignorance consciously or unconsciously.
8. Anyone preoccupied with greed or financial bondage.

9. Anyone who is or has been a practicing member of an organization or secret society or is involved in rituals, sacrifices, and demon worship disguised as gods.
10. Anyone who has undergone any form of initiation into the occult.
11. Anyone that experiences moving objects within their body.
12. Anyone in possession of totems by their ancestors and descendants.
13. Anyone experiencing nightmares.
14. Anyone experiencing suicidal or murderous thoughts.
15. Anyone practicing or has practiced any form of transcendental meditation.
16. Anyone relying on charms or crystals for protection.
17. Anyone using the Lord's name in vain or profanity.
18. Anyone who consults and worships angelic spirits.
19. Anyone obtaining anointing from cemeteries.
20. Anyone who has experienced astral projection or soul travel.
21. Anyone predisposed to operations of false signs and wonders.
22. Anyone who partakes of false doctrine, false prophets, false teaching, false ministries, and satanic ministers.

Always look to the Word of God for the truth!

23. Anyone who views their visions, prophecies, and dreams above the authority of the Scriptures.
24. Anyone being visited in dreams and mentored by spirit guides.
25. Anyone leaving their spouse to marry another claiming God authorized it.
26. Anyone knowingly entering an unequally yoked relationship with one who is not in a relationship with Christ.

Stop! Prayerfully consider the above!

A Controversial Matter

As stated earlier, whether one is in need of deliverance continues to be a controversial topic for some. However, after considering the above, I trust that you may be better able to assess your personal needs. If you have continued to struggle in a certain area of bondage without relief, this strongly suggests that you are in need of deliverance.

Again, the issue of a Christian having demons has raised much controversy. However, I must say that when one strongly denies this possibility, please consider this to be a *spirit of deception* that the devil is using to keep God's precious people from moving ahead effectively as God intends. Demons do not want to be discovered operating in our lives. They want to remain hidden so they can go about their tasks unhindered.

For those of us who have been set free and continue to be set free from demons after giving our lives to Jesus Christ, we know without a shadow of a doubt, that Christians can indeed have demons. I will shout this truth from the rooftops! *All are in need of deliverance* and for obvious reasons—the sooner the better.

There are clear indicators where deliverance is needed!

More Clear Indicators

1. The inability to break free from sinful habits.
2. A sense of being constantly harassed by evil spirits.
3. A conviction that you are not a good Christian because of guilt and perceived failures.
4. A lack of evidence of the fruit of the Holy Spirit in your life— love, joy, peace, long-suffering, goodness, gentleness, faith, meekness, and self-control.
5. Chronic sickness, disease, and illnesses without a cure.
6. Hereditary illnesses (asthma, cancer, diabetes, mental illness, heart disease, etc.)
7. Compulsive behaviors and disorders. Attraction to occult practices (séances, fortune telling, horoscopes, hypnosis, witchcraft, tarot cards, etc.)
8. Traumatic events that continue to torment.
9. Debilitating thoughts that cause emotional pain.

Stop! Do spend time and meditate on the above indicators.

Chapter Review!

1. Be sure you have a personal relationship with Jesus Christ before entering into the deliverance process.
2. Be sincere in wanting to be set free from every bondage.
3. Be willing to repent, renounce, and be released from all demonic activity.
4. If you don't believe you can have a demon, you are being deceived.
5. You can be totally set free through the deliverance process.
6. If you're struggling in some area and can't get the victory, you are probably in need of deliverance.
7. Identify areas that have given Satan an open door into your life and their source.
8. Use the authority God has given you over all the power of the enemy to cast out every unclean spirit so that you can experience personal freedom.
9. No longer allow the devil to afflict and torment you through ignorance of his devices.
10. Rise up with righteous indignation and declare "enough is enough"!

Stop! This chapter contains much truth.
Spend time in prayer and meditation!

Confession of Faith

Let's declare the following confession *out loud* together!

Father, I am so thankful to You for sharing with me the truth and for showing me that I can really be set free from the things that have held me captive. I will identify areas that have given Satan an open door into my life. With a spirit of power and authority, help me to learn what I need to do and how to do it so that I can be totally free from all torment and oppression. In Jesus's name, I pray. Amen.

Thou shalt preserve me from trouble; Thou shalt compass me about with songs of deliverance.

Psalm 32:7

In the next chapter, we will once again be discussing some things that you need to know that will better prepare you to go through the deliverance process.

Chapter 12

Expectations for Deliverance

*Behold, I send my messenger before thy face,
which shall prepare thy way before thee.*

Luke 7:27

Know Your Options

I trust that the following information will further assist you in being prepared for deliverance, and that you will better understand what may occur during the process. While deliverance can be initially a one-time event, generally, the need for deliverance continues throughout our *lifetime*. Why, because our adversary the devil continues to seek whom he can devour on a daily basis (1 Peter 5:8).

Press forward and receive all that is yours in Christ!

Although self-deliverance is an option, many times it may be necessary to seek the help from an experienced deliverance ministry. I encourage you to do just that when your need for deliverance is more *complex*. When this is the case, the deliverance session is another important option. However, through self-deliverance, we can successfully resist much oppression that the enemy brings our way on a daily basis. We will be talking more about this later.

The Deliverance Session

When self-deliverance is not enough, the deliverance session can make all the difference in setting you completely free. Some may experience freedom or a degree of freedom at once during the first session—while others may need a number of sessions. Often, one area may be addressed during one or more sessions, and others in future sessions. Many times, it takes multiple sessions before a person experiences a notable release.

Don't hesitate to seek additional help from those who are experienced deliverance ministers!

Sessions can range from a few minutes to several hours—depending on the needs that must be addressed. Nevertheless, do not allow yourself to become discouraged. Keep pressing forward to receive all that is yours in Christ—always keeping your focus on the work of the cross which has made your deliverance possible. The *deliverance team* usually consists of two to four individuals who act as deliverance ministers and intercessors.

Goal of Deliverance

Deliverance ministry is not simply casting out demons. There are also strongholds that need to be torn down that affect our mind, will, emotions, and physical bodies. This is done by the renewing of our mind according to the Word of God (Romans 12:2).

It is important to maintain a close relationship with the Lord to ensure ongoing deliverance!

I cannot stress enough the importance of maintaining a close *personal relationship* with the Lord which can keep the enemy from finding ways to torment you and your loved ones. Remember, the *purpose of deliverance* is to obtain freedom from everything that can hinder you from walking in the fullness of God's plan for your life and intimacy with Him.

Four Elements

Deliverance ministry can be divided into four areas of ministry. Let's review them together.

1. Determining areas in your life and the *source* which has given Satan the legal right to enter and remain.
2. Bringing down every *stronghold* affecting your soul and physical body.
3. Achieving inner healing from *traumatic experiences* as the Holy Spirit heals every wound in your soul.
4. Confronting and *casting out demons* after strongholds are destroyed and all legal rights canceled—commanding they go to uninhabited dry places (Matthew 12:43) which refer to the wilderness, waste places, and deserts.

Every area of oppression must be confronted and all legal rights removed!

Stop! Meditate on the four aspects of the deliverance ministry!

Demon Locations

In the process of confronting demons, it is important to know their names and locations in the physical body as much as possible—since demons will attempt to hide so that they can remain. Demons can be found in the mind, will, emotions, the conscience, memory, and different parts of the physical body— heart, blood, bones, brain, muscles, eyes, ears, tongue, and the various systems of the body— nervous, respiratory, endocrine, circulatory, and digestive.

Delivered from Depression

I trust a personal word of testimony will be helpful in this regard. During most of my life, I struggled with depression which I have learned since was a generational curse—handed down through my family ancestry. There seemed to be an ongoing sense of *heaviness* that I lived with day after day growing up. It didn't matter if life was going well or not. It seemed like a heavy

Be sensitive to what may be going on in your soul and body during deliverance ministry!

cloud would settle over me, sometimes for no apparent reason.

One day I would feel this oppressive heaviness and another I would not. I'm not talking about being down when stress and problems arise. This was different. However, as a result of learning about deliverance and the practice of self-deliverance as a way of life, I now resist this *negative emotion* and others—refusing to give place to demons that have tormented me for many years.

Since I have learned that heaviness is a demonic spirit as well as depression, I no longer give place to such torment (Ephesians 4:27). When we *understand the source* of many of our problems, we can be free as we practice self-deliverance and resist every attack of the enemy. Yes, when we know the truth by revelation from the Word of God and choose to walk in that truth, the truth will set us free (John 8:32).

Session Expectations

During a deliverance session, sometimes a demon may manifest while other times nothing happens when they are being cast out and expelled. Mild *manifestations* might include coughing, burping, spitting up, deep yawning, sighing, pressure, or pain in areas of the body and shaking. These should not be resisted but allowed to come forth. Sometimes a demon will speak through the one being delivered as well.

In this regard, well-known author and deliverance minister Frank Hammond, shared the following:

"In my own experience, as soon as I would address the demon, I would feel a pressure in my throat followed by coughing and bringing up phlegm. There would then be a perceptible release that the thing was out. Some individuals are able to accomplish this with greater confidence and aggressiveness than others.

Stronger manifestations can occur as well when a person is being delivered from severe oppression from occult involvement—satanism,

New Age practices, false religions, witchcraft, or other deeper demonic practices. Emotions may also manifest when demons are confronted and cast out such as spirits of grief, anger, or fear.

Sometimes spirits can be stubborn and require firmness in driving them out. Demons can *resist our authority* and therefore they require persistent pressure before they will cooperate. Nevertheless, when every *stronghold* is addressed and *legal rights* removed, every demon must obey when commanded in the name of Jesus. Failure to understand this truth can greatly hinder success in the deliverance process."

Stop! Time spent here reviewing is crucial!

Demonic Resistance

The enemy may often try to bombard you with doubts and fears, and make you feel like you will never be set free. Be prepared to fight those feelings as much as possible. It is important not to be afraid of demons. God is much more powerful, and His angels are here to

Some demons will resist being cast out more than others!

assist us! We may encounter some strong demonic spirits that will resist our authority. This is why we need to be *persistent!* Your freedom has been paid for by the *precious blood* of Jesus Christ, and we need to stand on that as we confront and battle the spirits at hand.

When demons are manifesting or being driven out, it is usually best not to do much talking. Spirits often leave through the mouth, and it is true that we can hold them back from coming out if we obstruct their passageway. If you feel something coming up your throat, don't try to stop it from coming out.

A Word of Caution

It is important to note here something that must be addressed and is often overlooked. Hanging on to your bondage can literally keep you from being delivered. It is important to let go and allow the demons to be released. For example, trying to remove a spirit of fear while

You play a very important part in the deliverance process!

you're choosing in your mind to hold on to fear will hinder your deliverance. However, being aware of this possibility can make all the difference.

Stop! Don't go on until you fully grasp this important truth!

Communicate What's Happening

Before beginning the deliverance process, you should fill out a "questionnaire" which will be very helpful in identifying *strongholds* and *root causes* that need to be recognized. I encourage you to take much time in completing the one that you will find at the back of the book. During this activity, take note of any uncomfortable feelings, nervousness, or shaking while trying to answer certain questions? If this is your experience, it is likely that certain demons in you are being aroused and do not wish to be discovered.

Here are some things you might wish to focus on that are quite common during a deliverance session and important to communicate to those ministering your deliverance.

1. The Holy Spirit may bring to your remembrance a past sin or situation that may have opened the door to demons.
2. Take note of any thoughts, emotions, or concerns you may have such as feelings of anger, fear, hate, rage, rebellion, or the desire to run out of the room.
3. Be aware of physical discomfort, pain, or pressure in your body. A headache may indicate a spirit is manifesting. Pain that moves around inside your body can indicate the presence of a demon.
4. You may experience confusion, racing thoughts rising up in your mind, and irrational emotions. Acknowledge a feeling of release when you sense departing demons leaving you.
5. Know that sometimes demons will try to go into hiding (to trick you into thinking they are gone).
6. Other times there may be additional spirits to be driven out. Nevertheless, maintain awareness of what is happening and communicate what you are experiencing.

Stop! Do review and meditate here once again!

Questions and Answers

Before going on to the next chapter, let's consider some answers to questions that contain important information. Remember, *reviewing* what you read over and over will help you to receive the revelation you need down in your spirit!

Question: Is my problem demonic?

Answer: Although all problems are not demonic, it is safe to say that there are many more caused by demons than most are willing to acknowledge. In general, you may need deliverance if you are still struggling after you have done all that you know to do, and still have obtained no relief with chronic illness or infirmities, emotional pain, ongoing torment and oppressive circumstances.

Question: How can I prepare for my deliverance?

Answer: Your part is very important. You must want to be set free and be willing to do the following: Fill out the questionnaire at the back of the book. Make a list of areas of torment and forgive all who have hurt you as you repent of bitterness and resentment. Repent and renounce all sin in your life past and present, and be aware of any strongholds as discussed in chapter eight. Ungodly soul ties must be broken as well as discussed in chapter ten.

Question: What spiritual weapons has God given to assist in deliverance?

Answer: The name of Jesus, the Word of God, and the blood of Jesus.

Question: What else do I need to reconsider to prepare for deliverance?

Answer: *Honesty* with yourself and God. Sin not confessed gives the enemy a legal right to remain. Ask God to reveal anything that is not of Him. "Search me O God and know my heart: try me and know my thoughts: And see if there be any wicked way in me" (Psalm 139:23).

Choosing to do all that you can will secure your full deliverance!

Humility that recognizes dependency upon God for your deliverance. "God resisteth the proud but gives grace unto the humble" (James 4:6).

Repentance that turns away from all sin and all evil. "Can two walk together, except they be agreed" (Amos 3:3)?

Renunciation that makes a clean break with Satan and all his works. "Many that believed came and confessed and shewed their deeds" (Acts 19:18).

Forgiveness of all who have wronged you in any way. "If ye forgive men their trespasses, your heavenly Father will also forgive you" (Matthew 6:14).

Prayer that asks God to deliver you in the name of Jesus. "Whosoever shall call upon the name of the Lord shall be delivered" (Joel 2:32).

Knowing the truth will set you free!

Warfare that confronts and commands demons to go in Jesus's name. "I give you power to tread on serpents and scorpions" (Luke 10:19).

Question: What can I expect when I am delivered?

Answer: Oppression will disappear, heaviness will lift, uneasiness will go, burdens will feel lighter, an inner sense of freedom and contentment, and the joy of the Lord will cause you to rejoice.

Question: Why is deliverance sometimes unsuccessful?

Answer: Lack of true repentance, failure to confess sins, failure to forgive, failure to renounce occult practices, failure to break ungodly soul ties, lack of willingness to cooperate, lack of true desire to be delivered.

Chapter Review!

1. The goal of deliverance is to achieve freedom on a daily basis from every attack of the enemy.
2. The need for deliverance is life-long because Satan will always seek to bring torment into your life in every way possible.
3. Self-deliverance can provide ongoing relief.
4. When self-deliverance is not enough, seeking others to assist you through the deliverance session may be needed for more severe cases of bondage.
5. Deliverance ministry seeks to identify legal rights that have been surrendered, strongholds that must be brought down, the inner healing of the soul, and confronting demons and casting them out.
6. An intimate relationship with the Lord Jesus is crucial in maintaining freedom from demonic oppression.
7. During the deliverance session, it is important that you cooperate fully and communicate what you may be thinking and feeling physically, mentally, and emotionally.
8. Demons can return after deliverance when they have the legal right to do so, and open doors remain through sin.

Stop! Spending much time in this chapter can make all the difference!

Confession of Faith

Let's make the following confession *out loud* together!

> Heavenly Father, thank you for preparing me with the knowledge I need to know in order to be completely set free. Give me Your strength, the will and the ability to do what I need to do to experience my deliverance and stay delivered. I know what You have done for others You will do for me as well, because with You all things are possible as I choose to believe. In Jesus's name, I pray. Amen.
>
> *Thou hast heard the desire of the humble: thou wilt prepare their heart, thou wilt cause thine ear to hear: To judge the fatherless and the oppressed.*
>
> *Psalm 10:17*

In the next chapter, we will be discussing the process of self-deliverance in detail, and the important part that you play in achieving the release you need.

Chapter 13

The Process of Self-Deliverance

Who delivered us from so great a death, and doth deliver: in whom we trust that he will yet deliver us.

2 Corinthians 1:10

Possessing Your Deliverance

I am so excited that you are now ready to experience self-deliverance for yourself, which is the main purpose of this writing—your being equipped to confront demonic spirits as needed and maintain freedom from all oppression. Remember, we said earlier that when you begin to address areas of bondage in your life, this activity of spiritual warfare is referred to as *personal* or *self-deliverance*.

Freedom from all bondage is yours to claim as you diligently practice self-deliverance!

Though the term "spiritual warfare" is more commonly used in the church today in resisting the devil (James 4:7), deliverance ministry also seeks to confront evil in the same way—only with the added intent of casting out demonic spirits from the physical body and soul.

Setting yourself and others free is not as difficult as one might expect. It has been my experience that God has purposely made His will and ways so simple to understand, that even a child can enter into all that is ours through Christ's work on the cross—and often does much more easily than adults.

I have come to appreciate the fact that it is I myself that has made my journey as a believer much more difficult than was necessary, due to the *lack of the knowledge* I needed in order to walk in divine health and deliverance.

Nevertheless, it is the cry of my heart to liberate all who are oppressed of the devil and are tormented in various ways. I have sought to share with you the truth about deliverance—trusting that the Holy Spirit will impart to your spirit the revelation that you must have so that you and those you care about can be set free and stay free.

The absence of the truth has caused many to suffer needlessly!

As previously discussed, as a believer, you have been given the power and authority to cast out demons from other people's lives as well as your own. Again, much of Jesus's ministry dealt with individuals who were terribly oppressed by the devil.

Today, it is a fact that many are bound and in need of deliverance from the forces of darkness. Unfortunately, the absence of *clear teaching* about deliverance has caused much unnecessary suffering to continue. Yes, the question remains, "Can a person deliver himself of demons and others as well?" Absolutely!

Nothing but the Truth

The truth is that we cannot keep ourselves free from demons, unless we engage in self-deliverance on a *regular basis*. This has been my experience and the experience of others! It is a battle we must be ready to engage in every day of our lives—as long as Satan and his kingdom have the freedom to attack and torment the people of God and all who inhabit the earth.

As a believer, you have the same authority as those who are active and called into full-time deliverance ministry. We have all been *commissioned* to set ourselves free and those around us. Jesus clearly promised those who believe, "In my name you shall cast out devils" (Mark 16:17).

Usually, a person only needs to learn how to practice personal deliverance—keeping in mind that *deliverance is a process*. It would be great if we could get rid of all our demons at once, and then forget about them for the rest of our lives—but this is not the case. However, through self-deliverance, we can live free of physical, mental, and emotional torment, and every form of bondage on a daily basis. Once again, this is my heartfelt prayer for you!

Stop! Do take time to meditate on the above.

Jesus Our Example

Although this may come as a surprise to you, according to Scripture, Jesus practiced deliverance every single day whenever confronted with evil and so should we—for He declared, "Behold, I cast out devils, and I do cures today and tomorrow, and the third day I shall be perfected and accomplish my purpose" (Luke 13:32).

Setting captives free was part of Jesus's everyday life!

It is important to note that Jesus demonstrated self-deliverance as well. (Matthew 16:21–23) relates that when Jesus began to tell His disciples that He must suffer many things and be killed, Peter rebuked Him saying, "Lord, this shall not be unto thee." But notice Jesus's response. "Get thee behind me, Satan: thou art an offence unto me: for thou savourest not the things that be of God, but those that be of men."

Here we see Jesus clearly resisting the devil as He spoke to the demon in Peter directly, who spoke through him. Satan was the source who used Peter, in this instance, to attempt to thwart the plan of God for all humanity. As our example, we too must daily rebuke any attempt of the enemy to deceive or bring torment into our lives or to use us to harm others (2 Thessalonians 2:3).

Stop! Meditate on this shocking revelation!

Deliverance for All

The *good news* is that all can be set free as we follow Jesus's example and practice deliverance *consistently*. A satanist, thief, murderer, liar, and adulteress can be set free in the *name of Jesus*. Deliverance can change your life and mine. You can stop doing things you don't want to do that you know are wrong, and that have brought torment to your life and others perhaps for years.

Remember, evil behavior is caused by demonic oppression or possession. Jesus knew this, which enabled Him to forgive those who tortured Him and nailed Him to a cross. Again, our problem is not with flesh and blood (people) but with principalities and powers, and rulers of darkness who often work through human beings—causing great suffering throughout the world (Ephesians 6:10–13). We've only to *exercise the power* and *authority* that is ours in Christ, and boldly rebuke, bind, and cast out evil when and wherever it manifests.

> *Stop!* Due to this immense truth, take as much time as you need to reflect once again!

Daily Warfare

It is clear from Scripture, why it is necessary to practice personal deliverance on a daily basis. Spiritual warfare and consistent resistance are necessary as you become more aware of demonic oppression.

Resisting demons should be practiced throughout the day!

I cannot stress this enough! Spiritual warfare is designed to be *offensive* and not defensive. Practicing self-deliverance means that if we are to live our lives free from all torment, we must aggressively confront every unclean spirit that tries to harass us in any way—whether it be in our mind, will, emotions, or physical bodies. We must bring every stronghold down and close every door that may give the devil the legal right to torment.

Prepare Yourself and Others

Apostle Guillermo Maldonado in his book *Inner Healing and Deliverance* has suggested that the following be kept in mind by all who intend to seek and practice deliverance. Action should be taken in these areas—which bear repeating. Let's revisit them as our study draws to a close.

Carefully consider and act upon each of the areas listed!

1. Make sure you are "born again". You will find a prayer for salvation at the back of the book to assist you if needed. Again, this is so important as previously discussed.
2. It must be your *sincere desire* to be set free, or deliverance will be unsuccessful. Be sure that you are fully committed to being set free from all that holds you captive.
3. You must be willing to *forgive all* who have hurt you and caused you pain and suffering. Without forgiveness, deliverance should be postponed until you are ready to forgive. Forgiveness is a decision we make and not an emotion.

4. You must be willing and ready to *renounce all sin* with a sincere heart of repentance—as you choose to turn away from all that is displeasing to God. Breaking bad habits, separating yourself from harmful relationships, surrendering your life to Christ, and maintaining a close relationship with God by spending time in His Word with prayer and fasting— need to become a way of life for you.

These steps must be implemented in order to achieve and maintain your deliverance!

5. Declare by confession to God that you want nothing to do with the devil and the kingdom of darkness—forsaking all past involvement with the occult and every hindrance as they may apply.
6. Take time to write down where you need deliverance and complete the *questionnaire* at the back of the book which will help you in this process.
7. Use a prepared list to assist you as you become aware of each demon by name. Command each demon to go in the name of Jesus as often as needed as you expel your breath forcefully.
8. *Confront* every unclean spirit as you become aware of them boldly. Address each demon or group of demons by name, commanding them to leave. It is very important that you always *speak out loud* during deliverance for your words are powerful and your weapons of warfare are mighty "for pulling down strongholds and every high thing that exalts itself against the knowledge of God" (2 Corinthians 10:4,5).

(The statement below will be of help to you in this process)

"Spirit of _____, I bind, rebuke, and cast you out in the name of Jesus. I give you no place in my life. You have to go and I forbid you from returning in Jesus's name."

Repeat as necessary until you experience a release, knowing that you have all power and authority over Satan and his kingdom.

(Use the list of "Demonic Spirits" at the back of the book to assist you.)

Stop! Begin to put into practice all of the above!

Additional Steps

1. Submit yourself to deliverance as often as necessary. It is best to first be delivered yourself, before attempting to deliver others.
2. Be baptized with the Holy Spirit. This will give you the power and discernment that you need during the deliverance process. According to (Acts 1:8) "You shall receive power when the Holy Spirit has come upon you." Declare the prayer below *out loud!*

When demons are cast out a void is created that must be filled by the Holy Spirit!

Pray: Lord Jesus, I ask you now to baptize me with Your Holy Spirit and with fire according to Your Word. I want to receive everything You have for me (Luke 3:16).

3. Use the weapons of warfare God has given you. Put on the whole armor of God (Ephesians 6:11–18). Use the name of Jesus (Philippians 2:10) and plead His precious blood over yourself, your family, loved ones, and all your possessions daily (Revelation 12:11).
4. Read and study the Word of God and pray regularly (Hebrews 4:12).
5. When spirits leave there will be a void created that needs to be filled by God. Pray the following prayer *out loud!*

Pray: Heavenly Father, thank you for your peace, love, and a sense of Your presence. I ask that every void that the spirits have left be filled now with Your Holy Spirit in the name of Jesus. Amen.

Stop! Review and meditate! Practice self-deliverance with determination and begin to teach others to do the same!

Daily Awareness

If we never sinned again, we would have no need for deliverance because as we have said, "Sin opens doors for demons to enter our lives." The biggest problem in practicing self-deliverance is in being able to *accurately identify* the spirits that are oppressing you at any given time. Most of us through the years have mistakenly considered demonic activity in our lives as our *own thoughts* and desires and mere expressions of our humanity. It is not uncommon for one when faced with the presence of an unclean spirit to think, "Oh, I thought that was just me."

This is why it is wise to experience an *initial deliverance* with an experienced minister if possible, before beginning to practice self-deliverance—especially when the level of bondage is severe. It's possible for a deceiving spirit or spirits to keep a person from seeing that there's anything wrong because he is unable to receive true discernment. However, you can also connect with another Christian or several believers, and minister deliverance with one another as you learn together and experience the process of self-deliverance. Nevertheless, for most, you can practice self-deliverance and be set free from much unnecessary torment as a way of life.

Experiencing Self-Deliverance

Basically, when you are troubled and feel tormented in some way, you need to recognize it for what it is, and deal with the demon or demons that are present—using the authority the Lord has given to you. Again, our purpose is always to remove all oppression by acknowledging its *source*, and then actively taking steps to resist all demonic activity that tries to enter your life.

Recognize demon spirits that are tormenting you and cast them out immediately!

Self-deliverance is experienced in the same way as with a deliverance minister—one who has been trained and is knowledgeable of the deliverance process. The only difference is that when you engage in self-deliverance, you are literally your own deliverance minister. You must actively seek to determine strongholds and possible open doors, and then *confront* any *demonic intruders*—binding, rebuking, and casting each demon out when discovered.

Recognize your Demons

Demons can manifest as a *thought* that suddenly appears in your mind causing you emotional pain. You may be reminded of a sin you've committed, a disappointment or failure, or traumatic event from the past. If you give place to this thought, you may start to feel sad, depressed, or even discouraged. What should you do?

Unfortunately, most do nothing! But because you know the truth now, you should immediately say *out loud*, (your words are powerful) "Oh, no you don't, devil. I bind, rebuke, and renounce that thought. I don't give place to that thought and I command you spirit of (depression, sadness, etc.) to go now to the "uninhabited dry places." (Some direct them to the pit or abyss) I forbid you from returning in the name of Jesus."

Remember, when you do this, as long as there is no legal right to stay, every demon must obey and depart. This should always be your *expectation*! Make sure there are no open doors or strongholds that need to be dealt with as we have previously discussed. (See chapters 7, 8, 9, and 10) Put into practice revelations you have received from the Word of God, and continue to use this *manual* as an important resource for your ongoing personal deliverance.

Always share your testimony with others, and give God the glory for the things He has done!

Healed of Arthritic Pain

I trust the following account will bring additional clarity as I share with you a personal experience with self-deliverance. How I handled this situation has become a way of life for me, and I pray will be for you as well.

A number of years ago, I awoke with severe pain in my left knee. When I tried to stand I could hardly walk. Like you, I had two choices: make an appointment to see my doctor and accept the pain, or I could immediately confront the pain and command it to leave. I chose the latter.

Yes, a battle ensued, but after four weeks of rebuking the spirits of infirmity, pain and arthritis, declaring the Word of God *out loud* and commanding my healing—one morning as I awoke, I discovered that all the pain was gone. I was miraculously healed (Isaiah 53:5).

Give no place to the devil ever again!

However, as can be expected, the enemy has tried to revisit this pain on several occasions, but has left soon after as I stood my ground and continued to *rebuke the devourer* (Malachi 3:11).

Today, knowing that healing, divine health, and deliverance are mine by inheritance in Christ, I give no place to any symptoms of illness, torment, or oppression of any kind. I have found that when I sternly rebuke the enemy time after time, *symptoms disappear* and unacceptable circumstances turn around. Be confident of this very thing—that this is the will of God for you as well.

What about You?

Should you have or begin to experience symptoms of illness or pain in your mind, emotions or physical body, or if your doctor has given you a diagnosis of some kind—because healing and deliverance are your divine right as a believer— never for a second accept that which is contrary to the Word of God. Begin spiritual warfare immediately—binding any spirits that you become aware of as you seek spiritual discernment from the Holy Spirit.

With experience, you will become more and more effective. Don't allow yourself to become discouraged or begin to question if what you are doing is really making a difference. In time, you will notice that there is less oppression as demons see that you are serious and will persist in casting them out.

Actively resist and cast out demon spirits that seek to oppress you and others!

Nevertheless, remember that we have been told in (1 Peter 5:8) "Be sober, (stay alert) be vigilant (very careful); because your adversary the devil, as a roaring lion, walketh about, seeking whom he may devour." "Neither give place to the devil" (a way for the devil to defeat you)" (Ephesians 4:27).

It is my prayer for you that the Holy Spirit will *impart this revelation* to your spirit—for when you act upon this truth, your life will never be the same!

Stop! You'll want to stop here and meditate.

Departing Demons

As mentioned earlier, when demons are cast out, *manifestations* will vary from person to person. Demonic manifestations differ because the personalities of demons vary. Some demons are passive and leave with no visible

Become familiar with possible manifestations that may occur when demons are expelled!

manifestation—while others may manifest strongly.

Some demons are very *stubborn* and resist being cast out. Some are talkative and boastful, while others are quiet and secretive. Most do not like to manifest because it usually results in their exposure and being driven out.

Demons tend to *act out their personalities.* So, for example, if you struggle with a temper or are afraid at times, casting out the spirits of anger and fear will bring relief. Or, if you are having a hard time forgiving someone, and you feel bitter and resentful, these spirits must be cast out as well. Be persistent in doing so, until your peace is restored and you have a sense of wholeness and well-being in your physical body, mind and emotions.

Sickness and Demonic Oppression

Today, it is important that we *grasp the revelation* that there are sicknesses directly connected to demonic oppression—demonic spirits that manifest in the form of common illnesses in the body and soul. The church must "awaken to this truth" so that all may experience total freedom from every form of torment and oppression.

Sickness can be directly connected to spirits of demonic oppression!

(Mark 9:17–29) confirms that there is a *direct correlation* between the ability to be healed and the need for deliverance. We are told in this passage that a boy was tormented by a mute spirit so that he was unable to speak, and who suffered greatly with seizures. This boy's sickness was a demonic manifestation of a deaf and dumb spirit and spirit of seizures. However, when Jesus cast out the unclean spirits, the boy was healed and set free from the torment he had endured since childhood.

Here we see that physical healing was manifested after demonic spirits were cast out. Could it be that the physical, mental or emotional condition you may be dealing with has as its source a demonic spirit or spirits as well?

Stop! Take a moment here and consider this possibility!

The fact is that if we are not aware of demonic activity in our lives—sickness, diseases, and infirmities are all too often embraced rather than resisted through the deliverance process. If you think that your sickness just came from your bloodline and is *hereditary*, it is likely that you won't use your authority over the demonic forces that may be behind your diagnosis. This is what the enemy wants you to do. *Nothing!*

The spirit of deception has kept many from walking in divine health and deliverance!

For far too long great deception has held many captive—believing that sickness was from God. Let's be clear! All sickness is from the devil. God may allow sickness for a number of reasons, which we have discussed, but as a loving Father He does not afflict His children any more than we would want to afflict ours.

The truth is that Satan's business is, and always has been, to afflict God's people with sickness and disease and every form of torment. For this purpose, Jesus came to earth so that He might destroy the works (business operations) of the devil (1 John 3:8).

Nevertheless, the *good news* is that self-deliverance when practiced correctly—will literally set you free. It is my great desire that you live a life free from all torment and bondage through personal deliverance.

Living free is possible and "yours for the taking." Whether we embrace this revelation is a decision each must make. We have been given the *power to choose* divine health and deliverance for ourselves. The evidence is abundant that the truths shared in this writing have resulted in the release of many captives—including this writer. May God give you the will and courage to step out in faith for all that is yours in Christ.

Rise up and possess all that has been purchased for you!

Stop! Let's take a moment to prayerfully reflect on what you have just read!

A Tormented Church

It is so important that the body of Christ, the church, receive this knowledge by revelation. For far too long, we have allowed the enemy to torment and oppress us without much resistance. There is no need for any believer to continue to suffer and be *held captive* any longer—when we have been given power and authority over all the power of the enemy (Luke 10:19).

Because the enemy opposes every "born-again" believer and desires to steal all that is ours in Christ, it is imperative that we grasp the truth by revelation from the Word of God today. It's time that we rise up and advance forcefully (Matthew 11:12) and possess all that has been purchased for us through Jesus's death on the cross. The sufferings of our Lord and Savior have obtained for us the promise of an eternal inheritance (Hebrews 9:15) which includes healing and deliverance.

Grasping this truth will set you free!

Self-Examination

For a moment, let's begin to look more closely at ourselves. Are there things in your life that you'd like to gain the victory over? Do you have a temper? Are you quick to judge others? Do you struggle with lustful thoughts or desires that are impure? Are you jealous of others? Are you often confused or do you struggle with doubt and unbelief? Are you depressed and discouraged much of the time? Do you feel inadequate, insecure, and afraid? Are you often sick with little quality of life and perhaps even have thoughts of suicide and death?

These are just a few examples of symptoms that you may be struggling with that are caused by unclean spirits whose *personalities* manifest in these ways. When this is the case, as a believer in Christ, you can have the victory through self-deliverance.

The Source of Your Problem

Though we struggle with many things throughout our lifetime, it may come as a surprise to you that a *tormenting spirit* may very well be the source of your problem. This truth came as a revelation to me a number of years ago as I began to study healing deliverance ministry.

Identifying the source of your problem is of major importance!

It's a wonderful thing to be free at last from all torment!

Whatever your need may be today, you can get rid of many unclean spirits that have held you captive through self-deliverance. Grasping this truth has literally set me free from much torment and oppression. As a believer, you too can take back what the enemy has stolen by using the power and authority God has given you through the name of Jesus and His precious blood. Again, this is the cry of my heart for you!

Stop! Take time to meditate as you consider your needs or those of a loved one!

Free At Last

Once again, you know you have been set free from demonic spirits when you are no longer doing what you know is wrong (stealing, lying, cursing, sexual sin, etc. or feeling painfully oppressed with harmful emotions such as fear, anxiety, depression, anger, jealousy, grief, etc.)

When you are aware of the demonic source behind many of your problems, personal deliverance can set you free!

Remember, it is the personality of every demon to want to continue to manifest in and through your life. Choose to be set free through the deliverance process.

Final Comments

As we close this chapter, if you haven't already done so as mentioned above, I'd like to suggest again that you make a list of all the things in your life you'd like to be set free from, and that you take the time to complete the questionnaire at the back of the book which will be of great help to you. Many times we are *consciously unaware* of a number of issues that we struggle with repeatedly. So again, do take ample time to complete this questionnaire. Should you choose to seek out experienced deliverance ministers, you can take it with you to share with them during your first session.

However, know that when applying the *time-tested truths* contained in this writing, self-deliverance is a very real option that can set you free. As you take steps to implement self-deliverance in your own life and teach others to do the same, the much needed awakening for healing deliverance ministry in the church can become a reality.

I truly pray that the Holy Spirit will take His truth concerning deliverance and impress it upon your spirit as revelation, and that having now spent much time seeking this truth, that you now feel enlightened and *empowered* to move forward in possessing your full deliverance.

Stop! Carefully review the chapter before
going on to the next!

Chapter Review!

1. Sickness can be caused by spirits of infirmity and disease.
2. Identify the source behind the problems you may be experiencing.
3. Self-deliverance can set you free from much torment and oppression.
4. Every believer should practice self-deliverance on a daily basis.
5. Manifestations may or may not occur during self-deliverance.
6. Spiritual warfare and consistent resistance are necessary to achieve freedom.
7. Claim the deliverance that was purchased for you on calvary's cross.

Confession of Faith

Let's make the following confession *out loud* together!

Lord Jesus, I truly rejoice in the knowledge You have given me so that I can walk in freedom from so much that has devastated me for so long. I look to You to help me act upon this truth each and every day, for myself and those I desire to help get set free as well. I embrace my deliverance and all that is mine in You. In Your name, I pray. Amen

And the Lord shall deliver me from every evil work, and will preserve me unto his heavenly kingdom: to whom be glory forever and ever. Amen.

2 Timothy 4:18

In the next and final chapter, we will discuss the need to carefully maintain our deliverance on a daily basis.

Chapter 14

Maintaining Your Deliverance

I will return to my house from whence I came out.

Matthew 12:44

Returning Demons

Demons will try to return so be alert!

As we have discussed, every believer in Christ has been given the power and authority to bind and cast out demons. Because of the real possibility of their return, we must learn how to maintain the freedom God has given to us on a daily basis.

Jesus set this example for us to follow. We read in (Mark 9:25) of an instance when Jesus forbid a deaf and dumb spirit from returning once it was cast out. In ministering to this man, Jesus said, "Thou dumb and deaf spirit, I charge thee, come out of him, and enter no more into him."

It is important for you to know which demons have been cast out so that you can be alert to their attempts to return—making sure there are no open doors which would give them the legal right. The issue of staying free from all demonic attacks is very important.

Scripture clearly states the possibility of demons returning to the life of a person after being cast out. It is a fact, that evil spirits can and do seek to return where they have been given access. They can be very deceptive. Jesus said,

> "When the unclean spirit is gone out of a man, he walketh through dry places, seeking rest, and findeth none. Then he saith, I will return into my house from whence I came out; and when he is come, he findeth it empty, swept, and garnished. Then goeth he, and taketh with himself seven other spirits more wicked than himself, and they enter in and dwell there: and the last state of that man is worse than the first" (Matthew 12:43–45).

Be aware that after you have experienced freedom in a certain area, an evil spirit may put a thought into your mind. This is a tactic of the enemy to deceive you into believing that you weren't really healed or set free at all. A return of symptoms of illness, painful emotions, or thoughts and wrong desirers might lead you to believe that a stronghold is still there when it is not. However, this attempt of the enemy must be *confronted immediately* as you have been taught.

Confronting demons is ongoing and life-long!

Requirements for Keeping Your Deliverance

The following will serve as a *review* and help us maintain our freedom. It is necessary that they become a "way of life" in order to stay free.

1. Develop a consistent *prayer life* (Matthew 26:41).
2. Read and *study the Word* of God. Meditate and confess what God's Word says and not what you may think, hear, or see (2 Timothy 2:15).
3. Separate yourself from all *unrighteousness* (Proverbs 1:15).
4. Daily *plead the blood* of Jesus which creates a circle of protection that the enemy cannot penetrate over every area of your life (Revelation 12:11).
5. Keep on the *spiritual armor* of God (Ephesians 6:10–18).
6. Develop a *forgiving spirit*. Bitterness attracts demons (Matthew 18:21–35).
7. *Resist the devil* with spiritual weapons—the name and blood of Jesus, the Word of God, fasting, and prayer (James 4:7).
8. Control your thought life by *casting down imaginations* and resist every lying thought that tries to return in the name of Jesus (2 Corinthians 10:4,5).
9. Forsake all *ungodly desires* of the flesh (Romans 8:4).
10. Live a lifestyle of *praise* and *worship* (Psalm 138:2).
11. Maintain *fellowship* with other believers (1 Corinthians 1:9).
12. *Surrender your life* to Christ as you purpose to live for Him (Romans 12:7).
13. Cultivate godly *covenant relationships* (1 John 1:7).
14. Maintain *strong faith* (Romans 10:17).
15. Use your *authority* in Christ (Matthew 16:19).
16. *Be aware* of areas Satan may try to recapture (1 Peter 5:8).
17. Keep a *humble spirit* (James 4:6).

Stop! Let's meditate on the above prayerfully!

Continue to Stand

Doing these things will insure that no demon will be able to return, much less bring others with him. However, if a demon should gain the legal right to *regain entrance* due to sin, after repentance, cast it out as soon as possible by yourself or with the help of other believers.

It is important that Jesus now rule in your life. If you should identify other areas of demonic activity at any time, remember, you have been given the authority over every demon spirit. Walk in daily deliverance and do *not settle for anything less!*

Never allow the enemy to torment or oppress you or those you love ever again. Consistent resistance will keep you and those dearest to you totally free. Yes, it is an ongoing battle, because the enemy is dedicated to your destruction. Nevertheless, you will find that as you continue to stand against every attack of Satan and his kingdom, once they see your *determination* to resist every assault, they will bother you less and less. However, always remember to obey the following admonition.

"Be sober, be vigilant; because your adversary the devil, as a roaring lion, walketh about, seeking whom he may devour: Whom resist steadfast in the faith, knowing that the same afflictions are accomplished in your brethren that are in the world" (1 Peter 5:8, 9).

Be determined and never settle for anything less than God's best!

Personal Responsibility

It is your personal responsibility to maintain your deliverance!

All too many have lost their deliverance because they were not instructed as to what to do afterward. When demons are expelled, the gifts (1 Corinthians 12:1-11) and fruits of the Holy Spirit (Galatians 5:22, 23) must replace them. This is our individual responsibility.

Demons despise the supernatural gifts of power and the fruits of the Holy Spirit, because when in operation, they counter the work of demons. When these power gifts are manifested, their plans to bring harm are thwarted. The *empowering* by the Holy Spirit is important in retaining your deliverance.

Nevertheless, maintaining deliverance is not based on sending demons away. There is much more involved in being free and staying free than having demons cast out. We cannot overemphasize this truth. Protection from demons returning is in being filled with the things of God. As we maintain *lives of repentance* from all sin and reject all satanic influences, we must then feed on the Word of God—always maintaining a forgiving heart.

Though others may encourage and help us stay free, it is the *personal responsibility* of each one of us to keep our deliverance on a daily basis. Always beware that after deliverance, Satan and his kingdom will continue to try and invade your thoughts, revisit painful circumstances, and symptoms of illness if allowed. This attempt must be resisted with all perseverance!

Stop! Prayerfully consider possible reasons why deliverance may become ineffective!

Incomplete Deliverance

What are some reasons why deliverance may fail or only result in a "partial deliverance"? Let's consider the following once again:

1. A lack of true repentance that does not change attitude and behavior.
2. Failure to confess sin.
3. A prideful spirit and unbelief.
4. Lack of true desire to be set free.
5. Unwillingness to forgive.
6. Failure to renounce occult involvement.
7. Unbroken ungodly soul ties.
8. Fear and embarrassment.
9. Failure to be completely honest.
10. Curses that remain unbroken.
11. Lack of biblical knowledge and spiritual discernment.
12. Legal grounds and open doors remain.
13. Failure to diligently practice self-deliverance.
14. Unwillingness to surrender all to the Lordship of Christ.

Stop! Meditate on the reasons deliverance may fail.

Beware of Deception

Should you once again open doors to demons from which you were delivered, there is no reason to hesitate seeking that freedom again. Continue to fulfill the above requirements for deliverance on a daily basis and persevere in maintaining self-deliverance as you become aware of any demonic oppression. Seek support from others as well as you maintain fellowship with other believers and never allow the devil to take what's yours in Christ. Never settle for less!

There is *no lasting benefit* from having demons cast out unless they are kept out. This is why it is important to learn how to stay free. The possibility of demons returning in greater force than when they left is *unacceptable*! We must remember that demons can do no more or less than we *allow* them to do.

Ongoing deliverance means entering into battle where your freedom will be tested over and over again. Just as Satan tested Jesus in the wilderness—know that the enemy will attempt to steal, kill, and destroy your freedom in Christ as well—anyway he can and as often as he can (John 10:10).

There must be strong *spiritual commitment* to stay free after initial deliverance in order to prevent further demonization from occurring. This again is why an unbeliever would be absolutely vulnerable. We must wisely teach those who are set free how to keep demons out *permanently*. Never let down your guard!

Returning demons are unacceptable!

Chapter Review!

1. Demons will try to return. Beware of *deception* and guard your thought life.
2. Revisit the list of things you must do to stay free and *practice* them as a way of life.
3. Maintain consistent *resistance* against any attempt of the enemy to steal your deliverance.
4. Should oppression return simply *repent*, close the open door, and be vigilant in casting out every demon every day.
5. Ongoing deliverance is *your responsibility*. Boldly use the authority that you have been given over all the power of the enemy.
6. Always be aware of those things listed above that can *hinder* your deliverance or prevent you from maintaining your freedom.

Confession of Faith

Let's make the following confession *out loud together!*

Lord Jesus, I rejoice that freedom from every attack of the enemy is mine to enjoy. Help me to be consistent and aware of Satan's tactics in advance, and to faithfully resist every attempt made against me and my family to bring torment and oppression. I purpose in my heart to do the things that will help me live free as a way of life. In Your name, I pray. Amen.

If the Son therefore shall make you free, ye shall be free indeed.

John 8:36

Epilogue

It has been my goal to equip you with the facts so that you can successfully put into practice the process of personal deliverance in your own life, and then go and take that knowledge and share it with others. Every believer has been commissioned to proclaim this truth through revelation from the Word of God.

If you will carefully meditate on the process of self-deliverance and put into practice the steps that we have discussed, you will experience the freedom that Jesus purchased for you through His sacrificial death on the cross.

By acknowledging the truth, your *faith to believe* that healing and deliverance are possible is a key principle that you must embrace. I cannot emphasize enough what Jesus said many times during the course of His healing deliverance ministry. "Be it unto you according to your faith" (Matthew 9:29), and "Your faith has made you well" (Luke 8:48).

I have sought to present to you the deliverance ministry, not just as an answer, but *the answer* to your deepest needs—a confident trust that declares that "with God all things are possible to those who will believe" (Luke 1:37). Though many continue to suffer beyond our comprehension, the healing deliverance ministry is God's gift to all *who are desperate* and in need of a miracle.

To be truly set free from the pain and torment that comes from the demonic realm, there are no words that can express the joy of release when one experiences freedom in Christ. Emptying Himself of His deity for a time, and taking upon Himself the form of a man, Jesus Christ took your sufferings in His own body at the whipping post and on the cross because of His great love for you—declaring you healed (Isaiah 53:5) and no longer held captive (Psalm 34:17).

We each have an important part to play in possessing all that is ours in Christ. Though *His work is finished*, ours is just beginning. We must secure for ourselves and our loved ones our salvation, healing, and deliverance from all that is evil. I earnestly pray as you take hold of "the truth" by revelation that your life will never be the same. Healing and deliverance are yours for the taking—but whether or not you partake is completely up to you.

Don't walk away unchanged after having read this book as we so often do. Visit and revisit its pages from time to time—until your faith becomes sight and your deliverance a reality. It's time that "the truth be told and shouted from the rooftops" (Matthew 10:27) for all to see and hear.

There is no greater gift that we could possibly give to the One who has made all this possible, than to be counted among those who are walking in the truth that sets us free. This is the Father's delight—to see His beloved living as overcomers, whole and prospering in every possible way—no longer a victim but a victor; no longer enslaved but liberated from the shackles of bondage to go forth as mighty conquerors—taking back all that the enemy has stolen.

Is this your heart's cry today as it is mine? Sound the battle cry, blow the trumpets, and leap for joy! Only when we are free can we truly enter into the joy of our Lord. Give testimony of the greatness of your God. Take Him at His Word—a glorious future beyond human comprehension awaits you. I say yes! Let it be so for the glory of our God—our Savior, Healer and Deliverer—Jesus Christ, and our soon coming King of Kings. Amen and Amen.

The Lord bless thee, and keep thee: The Lord make his face to shine upon thee, and be gracious unto thee: The Lord lift up his countenance upon thee, and give thee peace.
Numbers 6:24-26

List of Strongholds

Please note that the list below is not all inclusive, but rather consists of some of the *most common demonic spirits* that can affect our lives on a daily basis. As you seek to practice self-deliverance, you will want to refer to this list often. Many things that we have struggled with over a lifetime, have as their source unclean spirits who have sought to torment us and ultimately destroy us.

Pride	Slumber
Perfection	Withdrawal
Accusation	Mind Binding
Competition	Sleepiness
Mockery	Forgetfulness
Self-Righteousness	Stupidity
Fear of Authority	Insomnia
Boastfulness	Trances
Sarcasm	Laziness
Panic Attacks	Jealousy
Gluttony	Lethargy
Addictions	Sluggishness
Deafness	Confusion
Procrastination	Divination
Insanity	Magic
Fear	Murder
Inadequacy	Word Twisting
Inferiority	Familiar Spirit
Timidity	Spirit Guides
Worry	Witch/Warlock/Satanist

Sensitivity	Indian Curses
Gossip	Santeria
Torment	Roots Curses
Nightmares	Voodoo Curses
Greed	Word Curses
Anxiety	Guilt
Nervousness	Self-Pity
Abandonment	Loneliness
Bulimia	Depression
Seizures/Epilepsy	Manic Depression
Doubt and Unbelief	Suicide
Rebellion	Prostitution
Witchcraft	Covetousness
Self-Exaltation	Fornication
Stubbornness	Religious Spirit
Poverty	Impatience
Terror	Bitterness
Hindering Spirit	Emotional Weakness
Criticalness	Homosexuality
Phobia	Retaliation/Wrath
Obesity	Sodomy
Anorexia	Sensual Thoughts
Mental Illness	Anger
Infirmities	Rage
Heaviness	Hatred
Double Mindedness	Violence
Multi-Personality	Restlessness
Arthritis	Selfishness
Despair	Condemnation
Grief	Lying
Gloominess/Sadness	Deception

Hyperactivity	Cancer
Self-Mutilation	Death
Fatigue	All Diseases
Allergies/Asthma/Hay Fever	Pain
Rejection	Fever
Inherited Curse	Daydreaming
Insecurity	Cult
Seducing Spirit	Adultery
Isolation	Revenge
Exaggeration	Suspicion
Vanity	Legalism
Profanity	Idolatry
Hypocrisy	Strife
Theft	Occult
Lesbianism	Perversion
Control	Lust

List of Generational Curses

Below you will find those that are most common:

Alcoholism	Drugs
Incest	Abortion
Homosexuality	Diseases
Chronic Sickness	Violence
Sexual Immorality	Greed
Child Molestation	Imprisonment
Premature Deaths	Accidental Deaths
Physical Abuse	Emotional Abuse
Nicotine	Addictions
Divorce	Suicide
Murder	Fornication
Insanity	Adultery
Mental Illness	Poverty
Pornography	Financial Problems
Marital Problems	Miscarriages
Accidents	Rebelliousness

Demon Groupings

Demons are identified according to their nature. Each is a specialist, and they are seldom found alone. They are together in groups. Such groups may be referred to as colonies or families. When one is detected, be alert to look for its companions. A group of demons may band together for the purpose of controlling a particular area of a person's life. Therefore, there is a very logical pattern of spirits to be found in many groups.

Within each grouping there will be a strongman or ruling spirit. Here are some common demon groupings. There is a leader or *strongman over each group* though they can vary from person to person. You will notice that when one is present, usually the others in the group will be as well.

<u>Bitterness</u>: resentment, hatred, unforgiveness, violence, temper, anger, retaliation, and murder.

<u>Insecurity</u>: inferiority, self-pity, loneliness, timidity, shyness, inadequacy, and instability.

<u>Depression</u>: despair, despondency, discouragement, defeatism, dejection, hopelessness, and suicide.

<u>Rebellion</u>: self-will, stubbornness, disobedience, unsubmissiveness, and dissension.

<u>Jealousy</u>: selfishness, suspicion, envy, distrust, and rivalry.

<u>Pride:</u> vanity, ego, haughtiness, self-righteousness, arrogance, and discord.

<u>Addictions</u>: nicotine, alcohol, drugs, medications, caffeine, and food.

<u>Lust</u>: fantasy, masturbation, homosexuality, adultery, fornication, and incest.

<u>Control</u>: possessiveness, dominance, witchcraft, and manipulation.

<u>Worry</u>: fear, anxiety, dread, and apprehension.

<u>Guilt:</u> shame, condemnation, unworthiness, and embarrassment.

<u>Passivity</u>: listlessness, indifference, and lethargy.

<u>Indecision</u>: procrastination, compromise, confusion, and forgetfulness.

<u>Cursing</u>: gossip, blasphemy, criticism, and backbiting.

<u>Gluttony:</u> nervousness, compulsive eating, frustration, idleness, and self-pity.

Grief: sorrow, heartache, heartbreak, crying, sadness, and isolation.

Carnality: control, envy, jealousy, fantasy, pride, and lust.

Deliverance Prayers

Prayer to be Born Again

Lord Jesus, I come to You with a repentant heart. I believe that You are the son of God and that you died on the cross for my sins and rose again from the dead. I renounce all my sins and those of my ancestors, and I submit myself to You as my Lord and Savior. I want to live for You from this day forward and fulfill Your plan for my life. Amen.

Prayer for Release

Lord Jesus, by a decision of my will, I forgive all who have hurt me in any way, just as You have forgiven me. I renounce all contact with the occult or satanic involvement, past or present, and I cancel all legal rights that I have given to Satan.

Because You took upon Yourself every curse for me, I now release myself from all that is evil and all spiritual wickedness. By faith, I thank You that every curse over my life has been revoked and canceled.

I thank you and declare that Satan has no more claim against me or my family, and from now on as I walk in obedience to Your will, your blessings will come upon me and overtake me. I believe and receive every blessing that you have for me and those for which I am praying in Your name. Amen.

Warfare Prayer

Heavenly Father, I come to You in the name of Your son, Jesus, and I ask you to forgive me for everything I have done to displease You in any way. Cover me with the precious blood of Jesus and fill me with Your Holy Spirit. Give me Your thoughts and desires as I surrender my will to You. Keep me on the path that You have chosen for me, and show me Satan's tactics in advance.

I put on the whole armor of God, and I pray that every thought that Satan or any demonic spirit tries to put in my mind will bounce off the helmet of my salvation and return to the sender. Heal every memory or circumstance that could hold me back from being all that You want me to be.

I recognize that I have on Your breastplate of righteousness; my loins are girded with the truth and my feet carry the preparation of the gospel of peace. I take up the sword of the spirit which is the Word of God and my shield of faith.

For myself and all the people I am praying for today, I ask You to draw us to Yourself, convict us mightily of our sins, keep us from temptation, deliver us from evil and cover us with the blood of Jesus. Send Your angels to keep us from any kind of accidents, harm, injuries, illness, death, destruction, disease, or pain.

Bind our marriages and our families together and make us one in You. If there is anyone in our lives that You do not approve of, I ask You to move them out and bring in those that You do approve of. Bless every area of our lives so that we can serve You according to Your perfect will in Jesus's name.

Satan, I come against you and your entire kingdom, and I declare that you cannot have any part in our lives. You can have nothing to do with our minds, bodies, souls, spirits, emotions, and wills; our marriages, finances, relationships, and ministries in Jesus's name.

I now break the power of every curse spoken or written against us, and I reverse each curse and send it back to the demon that brought it in the first place. I command every demon go bound into the uninhabited dry places and never return, and I break every ungodly emotional soul tie that is connected to any one of us in the name of Jesus.

Through the living blood of Jesus Christ, I bind and sever every cord of any prince or principality, strongman, and every spirit of darkness, and I put Jesus's blood between every one of you. I cut off your communications and confuse your camp. I declare you inactive, and I cast you out in Jesus's name.

I bind and cast out every unclean spirit of poverty, lack, confusion, mind binding, anxiety, fear, heaviness, jealousy, bondage, whoredom, lying, perversion, and infirmity. I plead the blood of Jesus around our properties, and I bind you Satan and your entire kingdom from crossing that bloodline. You can have nothing to do with any one of us or any aspect of our lives. Heavenly Father, I now call on Your warring angels to make it happen.

Satan, I take authority over you and command you and all your evil spirits to loose our possessions. I demand that you restore every loss, seven-fold in Jesus's name.

I ask You Father to send Your warring angels and cause to come into our families all the assets and things Satan has stolen from us that have been ours through the blessings of Jesus Christ.

I now loose myself and those that I am praying for to the power of the Holy Spirit, and I speak forth blessings of prosperity, wisdom, revelation, discernment, abundance, and divine health. I declare we have a sound mind and reject every evil thought and receive every good thought. I loose myself and those I love to the ministry of the Holy Spirit, and I speak the fruit of the Holy Spirit into our lives—love, joy, peace, long-suffering, gentleness, goodness, faith, meekness, and self-control.

Satan, I declare that you and your entire kingdom cannot and will not hinder from coming to pass any prophecy of God that has been spoken over me, my family, and everyone that I am praying for today. Father, once again I ask You to dispatch Your mighty warring angels to go on our behalf to make sure that every godly prophecy spoken over us comes to pass in Jesus's name. Amen.

A Prayer for Healing and Deliverance

Heavenly Father, thank you for giving me authority over Satan and every demonic spirit. Thank you for giving me the authority to bind and loose. Devil, according to Scripture my Father has given me authority over you, to cast you out, to bind you, and cause you to flee (James 4:7). Being fully submitted to God I resist you now and you must go in the name of Jesus.

Spirits of sickness, disease, infirmities, and pain, I bind you and command you to leave and I forbid you from returning. I now loose divine health and deliverance from all torment and oppression, and I thank you, Father, for my healing miracle and complete deliverance in the name of Jesus Christ. Amen.

Prayer to Renounce Ungodly Soul Ties

Thank you Lord Jesus for dying that I might be set free from every harmful thing in my life. I invite You to be the Lord of my life and I ask You to set me free. I confess and repent of all my sins, and I forgive and loose those with whom I have had an ungodly relationship.

I now break and renounce every ungodly soul tie (name each person). With the authority given to me in Jesus Christ, I command all demonic spirits that entered my life through these relationships to leave me now in Jesus's name (name each spirit). Amen.

Prayer for Sevenfold Return

I command you Satan and your entire kingdom to return to me sevenfold everything that you have stolen—including my time, finances, relationships, health, well-being, and every spiritual blessing.

Father, dispatch your angels to make sure everything is returned immediately. I speak prosperity and favor over my life now in Jesus's name. Amen.

Prayer to Break Curses

Heavenly Father, I come to you with a heart of repentance, and I ask you to forgive me for all my sins. I also renounce the sins of my ancestors. I now break and loose myself and my family from all hereditary curses, and all demonic bondages placed upon us as a result of sin.

I renounce Satan and all his evil works and take back all that I have given to him. I give you no place and declare that you have no power over me. I belong to God and will serve Him only. By the authority of Jesus Christ I break the power of every evil curse that has come upon my life. I command every demon of curse to leave me now in the name of Jesus (name each curse).

(Now name and renounce each curse using the examples below. (See Section: "List of Generational Curses")

Cancer, I renounce and break your power over my life and curse every cancerous cell in my body at its roots in Jesus's name.

I break and renounce the *curse of poverty* over my family and declare prosperity and financial blessings in every area of our lives in Jesus's name.

I break and renounce the *curse of divorce* and bind the enemy from destroying marriages in my family and every family. I declare blessings over every member and the fruit of Your Holy Spirit—love, joy, peace, long-suffering, kindness, goodness, faithfulness, gentleness, meekness and self-control in Jesus's name.

I break and cancel the *curse of pornography* in the name of Jesus.

Prayer of Protection

Heavenly Father, I am so grateful for Your abiding presence and Your many promises that are found in Your Word. I pray for Your protection for myself, my family, and all those I make mention of today.

I declare every curse null and void and every evil spirit be bound and cast out in the name of Jesus. (name each one). Send Your ministering angels to guard and protect all of us, and I thank you for a hedge of protection that You have placed around us to keep us in all our ways. In the name of Your dear son Jesus, I pray. Amen.

Prayer for Baptism of the Holy Spirit

Lord Jesus, I want everything You have for me. Thank You for saving me and forgiving all my sins. I ask You to baptize me with the Holy Spirit and fire so that I will have the power and all that I need to serve You in the days to come. I receive my heavenly prayer language, which I now speak forth by faith out loud. Thank You for this precious gift. In Your name I pray. Amen.

Deliverance Questionnaire

Answering the following questions will be of great help to you in determining those areas where deliverance is needed. Since demons must have "legal consent" to enter your life, it is our purpose to identify those *doorways* which gave them that freedom.

The fact is once *permission* is granted, demons take up residence in the soul and physical body, and they do not have to leave if they have consent to stay. It is important to determine what permission they may have been given.

Where there is no forgiveness, a lack of repentance or surrender in a believer's life, demons do not have to leave. However, if all legal rights are canceled, then they must be obedient to do so in the name of Jesus. (Review: Chapter 8, "Strongholds")

It is important that every demon spirit be *identified* in order to receive the freedom that you desire. Where a choice is given, circle all that apply.

1. Have you been born again? Describe how and when you became a Christian.

   _____
   _____
   _____

2. Describe your relationship with your father. Positive or Negative?

   _____
   _____

(Circle all that apply) Kind or harsh? Supportive? Distant? Abusive physically or verbally? Fair or unfair? Strict or permissive? Proud or critical of you? Mistreated or well taken care of?)

3. Describe your relationship with your mother. Positive or Negative? What words would you use to describe your mother?

4. How would you describe your parents' relationship? Good or Bad? Divorced or Remarried? Stepparents?

5. Describe your relationship with brothers or sisters. Did you get along? Yes or No?

6. Discuss how you feel about your family.

7. Describe relationships in school.

   Teachers?

   _____
   _____
   _____
   _____
   _____

   Friends?

   _____
   _____
   _____
   _____

8. Describe military service. Good or Bad?

   _____
   _____
   _____
   _____

9. Describe employment experiences. Good or Bad?

   _____
   _____
   _____
   _____

10. Describe relationship with a spouse/s.

    _____
    _____
    _____
    _____

11. Occult Involvement: (Circle) (ouija board, fortune telling, horoscopes, tea leaves, tarot cards, palm reading, séances, mediums, spiritists, yoga, martial arts, possession of indian, african, or oriental objects) Other?

_____
_____
_____

12. Sex Outside of Marriage: Yes or No (Circle) (Lust, Pornography Abortion, Incest, Rape, Sexual Perversions) Other?

_____
_____
_____
_____

13. Involvement: (Circle) (Drugs, Alcohol, Addictions) Explain:

_____
_____
_____
_____

14. Traumatic Experiences: Yes or No?
    Explain:

_____
_____
_____
_____

(Circle) (Fears, Nightmares, Hearing Voices, Mental Disorders, Other?)
Explain:

_____
_____
_____
_____

15. Personal Qualities: (Circle)

(Perfectionist, Workaholic, Critical, Proud, Manipulative, Controlling, A Worrier, Nervous, Lazy, Unreliable, Liar, Thief, Gossip, Confused, Timid, Rejected, Depressed, Hopeless, Suicidal, Jealous, Boaster, Complainer, Dishonest, Glutton, Greedy, Selfish, Shy, Self-righteous, Self-pity, Habits, Addictions, Angry, Exaggeration, Need to please others, Procrastination, Sense of failure, Inadequacy, Insecurity, Intimidated, Fearful, etc.)

Bibliography

Banks, Bill and Sue. *Breaking Unhealthy Soul-Ties.* Kirkwood Missouri: Impact Christian Books. 2006.

Bridges, Kynan. *Possessing Your Healing.* Shippensburg, Pennsylvania: Destiny Image Publishers. 2014.

Bubeck, Mark I. *The Adversary.* Chicago, Illinois: Moody Bible Institute of Chicago. 1975.

Dickerman, Don. *When Pigs Move In.* Lake Mary, Florida: Charisma House. 2009.

Hammond, Frank. *Demons and Deliverance: In the Ministry of Jesus.* Kirkwood, Missouri: Impact Christian Books. 2007.

Hammond, Frank and Ida Mae. *Pigs in the Parlor.* Kirkwood, Missouri: Impact Christian Books. 2008

Hammond, Frank and Ida Mae. *The Breaking of Curses.* Kirkwood, Missouri: Impact Christian Books. 2009

Hollis, Paul and Claire PhD. *Exposing and Expelling Strongholds.* Tampa, Florida: Warfare Publications. Revised 2000.

Jackson, John Paul. *Needless Casualties of War.* Fort Worth Texas: Streams Publications: 1999.

Lozano, Neal and Janet. *Unbound.* Clinton Corners, New York: Attic Studio Publishing. 2008.

MacNutt, Francis. *Deliverance from Evil Spirits.* Grand Rapids, Michigan: Chosen Books. 2009.

Maldonado, Guillermo. *Inner Healing and Deliverance.* Miami, Florida: ERJ Publications. 2007.

New American Standard Bible. Lockman Foundation. 1960, 1995.

New King James Version. Thomas Nelson, Inc. 1982.

Phillips, Ernie and Betsy. *Charge!* Cheektowaga, New York: Communion with God Ministries. Revised 1992.

Prince, Derek. *They Shall Expel Demons.* Grand Rapids, Michigan: Derek Prince Ministries International. 1970.

Prince, Derek. *Blessing or Curse.* Grand Rapids, Michigan: Chosen Books. 2003.

Robeson, Drs. Jerry and Carol. *Strongman's His Name.* New Kensington, Pennsylvania: Whitaker House. 1984.

The American Heritage Dictionary of the English Language. Houghton Mifflin Company. 2009.

The Amplified Bible. Lockman Foundation. 1987.

The Full Life Study Bible. Grand Rapids, Michigan: Life Publishers International. The Zondervan Corporation. Division of Baker Publishing Group. 1995, 2006.

About the Author

Mary Ellen Gordon seeks to live in the realm of the supernatural where miracles are a normal part of everyday life. She is committed to "miracle ministry" with a passion and compassion to see all who suffer, be healed and totally set free for the glory of God!

Having received a mandate from the Lord, "Let the Truth Be Told! Shout It from the Rooftops!" she is taking the Full Gospel of Jesus Christ around the world as she teaches the Body of Christ how to walk in the miraculous—divine health, wholeness, and freedom from every form of bondage.

Ordained as a minister of the gospel of Jesus Christ through *Full Gospel Assemblies*, Parkesburg, Pennsylvania, she is the president and founder of *Waves of Glory Miracle Ministries*, located along Lake Erie in Western New York. She has launched a radio ministry, *Here Comes a Miracle*, where she shares what God is doing supernaturally here and around the world— always reminding her listeners that "truly with God nothing is impossible, and God has a miracle for you, today."

She is also the author of *Believe and Receive Your Miracle, Today* stating that her first two books contain the simple truth which will enable you to experience the saving, healing, and delivering power of God—which will change your life forever.

She openly declares that anything less is unacceptable, and that it's time that "the church" as we know it today, walk in the *supernatural power* of God as it fulfills the "Great Commission"—confirming the Word of God with signs and wonders.

Pastor Gordon is available for miracle seminars, conferences, and miracle services upon request by contacting:

Waves of Glory Miracle Ministries
1610 Old Manor Drive, Derby, NY 14047

E-mail: *waveofgloryministry@gmail.com*
Website: *wavesofglorymiracleministry.wordpress.com*

If the Son therefore shall make you free,
  ye shall be free indeed.

John 8:36

www.ingramcontent.com/pod-product-compliance
Lightning Source LLC
LaVergne TN
LVHW021818060526
838201LV00058B/3432